Davenport's New York Wills And Estate Planning Legal Forms

DAVENPORT'S NEW YORK WILLS AND ESTATE PLANNING LEGAL FORMS

2024 EDITION

written by attorneys
Alex Russell and Robert Maxwell

SEE BOOKS AND LEGAL FORMS AT WWW.DAVENPORTPUBLISHING.COM

COPYRIGHT © 2024 -- ALEX RUSSELL

CREATIVE COMMONS LICENSE. This work is also licensed under a Creative Commons Attribution-NonCommercial-NoDerivatives 4.0 International License.

GOVERNMENT WORKS. No claim is made to copyright or ownership of government materials.

SOME STANDARD FORMS. No copyright or ownership is claimed of "standard" forms or leading forms for the state which are provided in this book, but fair use and privilege to use is claimed. Makers of such forms (often a state agency or hospital) have agreed by word, act, and implication the forms may be used and copied if no profit is sought and no substantial changes made to them. Such makers if not a lawyer or law firm are barred from profit or advantage in practicing law by making forms then limiting use. Forms and other related materials are used here for educational purposes only. Authors strongly believe in a religious duty to help people and do charity.

PUBLICATION DATA
(informal, library may use different data)

Names: Russell, Alex, 1972- author; Maxwell, Robert, 1960- author

Title: Davenport's New York Wills And Estate Planning Legal Forms 2024 Edition

Other Titles: Davenport's Wills

Description: Davenport Publishing 2024

Suggested Identifiers: 9798362633165, LCCN 2021909030, 9798748423373

Subjects: LCSH: Wills--United States;
　　　　　　　　　Wills--United States--Forms;
　　　　　　　　　Estate Planning--United States;
　　　　　　　　　Legal Forms

Classification: LFF KF755 .C55 2024 (or as library chooses)
　　　　　　　　　DDC 346.73 Rus--dc24 (or as library chooses)

9 8 7 6 5 4 3 2 1 0 0 0 0 0 2 4

PERMISSION TO COPY AND USE BOOKS FOR FREE

To help people and groups publisher and authors of the book allow mostly free use by giving all a "Creative Commons Attribution-NonCommercial-NoDerivatives 4.0 International License".

Basically as image below shows copying or use is OK if it still shows it's **by** the named authors, is **non-commercial** with no price charged, and has **no derivatives** which means no big changes.

Most users face no limit on copying, using, holding in library to loan out, or giving out copies.

Permission is given to change margins and formatting, do small changes, and cut any blank pages that may occur (but double-check page numbers and table of contents page numbers).

Printing on only 1 side of pages avoids complication of writing on back. Text margins are .75 inches. To do a book not a pamphlet increase left (inside) and decrease right (outside) margins.

Users can design a cover they like but the book title and author names must still appear on it.

Email questions to **davenportpress@gmail.com**.

(This work licensed under a Creative Commons Attribution-NonCommercial-NoDerivatives 4.0 International License.)

FOR FREE COPIES USE WWW.DAVENPORTPUBLISHING.COM OR BUY AT AMAZON.COM.

WARNING

THIS PUBLICATION IS NOT A SUBSTITUTE FOR LEGAL ADVICE. Publisher and authors say and warn this publication is not giving any legal, accounting, or other professional services or advice, which if wanted can be obtained by consulting in person an attorney or some other professional. **No attorney-client relationship or any relationship creating a duty or obligation is agreed to or created by the purchase or use of this publication or forms.**

BOOKS AND FORMS FOR OTHER STATES ARE AVAILABLE, SEE WWW.DAVENPORTPUBLISHING.COM FOR INFORMATION

CHAPTER	TABLE OF CONTENTS	PAGE NUMBER
CHAPTER 1 - LIST OF LEGAL FORMS AND BOOK BASICS		1
CHAPTER 2 - TERMS, PROPERTY, AND HELPFUL INFORMATION FORM		4
CHAPTER 3 - WILL BASICS		8
CHAPTER 4 - WILL GIFTS INCLUDING RESIDUE CLAUSE		11
CHAPTER 5 - DEBT, MARRIAGE, AND YOUNG CHILD ISSUES		16
CHAPTER 6 - BASIC IDEAS ABOUT HEALTH CARE FORMS		19

WILL RELATED FORMS

CHAPTER 7 - FORM 1: LAST WILL AND TESTAMENT (STANDARD)		20
CHAPTER 8 - FORM 2: LAST WILL AND TESTAMENT (GUARDIAN)		24
CHAPTER 9 - FORM 3: SELF-PROVING AFFIDAVIT		28

HEALTH CARE FORMS

CHAPTER 10 - FORM 4: HEALTH CARE PROXY		30
CHAPTER 11 - FORM 5: LIVING WILL		39
CHAPTER 12 - FORM 6: DO NOT RESUSCITATE		43

GIVING POWER FORMS

CHAPTER 13 - FORM 7: STATUTORY SHORT FORM POWER OF ATTORNEY		50
CHAPTER 14 - FORM 8: DESIGNATION OF PERSON IN PARENTAL RELATIONSHIP		58
CHAPTER 15 - FORM 9: APPOINTMENT OF AGENT TO CONTROL DISPOSITION OF REMAINS		67
APPENDIX: FILLED OUT SAMPLE LEGAL FORMS		70

CHAPTER 1
LIST OF LEGAL FORMS AND BOOK BASICS

ESTATE PLANNING MOSTLY IS DOING SIMPLE THINGS IN 3 AREAS

This book helps people in New York do legal documents to control their property, money, children, health care, funeral, and more if later they are absent, sick, or dead. Doing this is usually called "Estate Planning". This book has about 9 ready to use legal forms in 3 areas, but most people use just a few of these forms.

WILL RELATED FORMS

Form 1. Will (Standard) – a Will (also called a "Last Will And Testament") lets a person control things after their death like who gets money and property, who is Executor, and if easier legal options can be used.

Form 2. Will (Guardian) – Will with part added to name a person to be Guardian to care for a minor child under 18 if needed (like if both parents later die) and also manage a minor child's property and money.

Form 3. Self-Proving Affidavit – optional form done with a Will to later help show it was signed right.

HEALTH CARE FORMS

Form 4. Health Care Proxy – this popular form lets a person in case they are incapacitated later so can't control things directly name someone to control health care and, also, write health care instructions.

Form 5. Living Will – does serious action of saying to not provide medical care if later the doctors think an incapacitated person is in very bad health and more care likely won't help.

Form 6. Do Not Resuscitate – these are really 2 forms that do serious act of immediately refusing health care, and these are short so paramedics can read them fast so they can be used outside any care facility.

GIVING POWER FORMS

Form 7. Statutory Short Form Power Of Attorney – lets power over money, property, and more be shared during life with someone named like a spouse or friend so they can do things to help.

Form 8. Designation Of Person In Parental Relationship – lets a parent share power over a child under age 18 with someone so they can help and make decisions about health care, school, and discipline.

Form 9. Appointment Of Agent To Control Disposition Of Remains – lets a person be named to control funeral and related matters, and this is done only if a person doesn't want closest family to do this.

NEW YORK LAW ON ESTATE PLANNING COVERS MOST PEOPLE HERE

This book is only for New York state since Estate Planning laws and legal documents vary between states. <u>Usually a state's Estate Planning law applies if a person's primary residence is here</u> (called their "domicile"). Many judges say "residence" occurs if a person lives in a place and has no clear plans to leave. Later plans to move don't matter till people move. <u>People can stay under a previous state's Estate Planning laws after they move</u> if people always plan to leave a new state. For example, people who move to a new state for years or more for travel, school, work, or military may keep legal ties to their old state. <u>Many people do health care forms for the state a health facility is in</u>. Most immigrants of any kind can do Estate Planning here.

PERSON HAS POWER TO CONTROL THESE THINGS BUT IT'S OFTEN NOT VITAL

Estate Planning to control health care, property, money, children, funeral, and similar things if a person is absent, sick, or dead is usually easy to do since by law a person mostly has full power to control these things. Given this usually judges, doctors, and other people mostly just ask: <u>"Based on what a person wrote what did they likely want done?"</u> Estate Planning is also easy because simple legal documents can mostly do things and simple words can be used (like putting a few names and listing some property). Note, despite what many people think Estate Planning is often not worth spending a lot on since it often does not greatly change the costs, taxes, delays, and later work in these areas. Benefits seem especially low for young people since just 4% of people die by age 50, and only 0.2% of children before age 18 have 2 parents die to need legal help. *See Social Security Standard Tables by Felicitie Bell*; *Parent Mortality Census SIPP Study Paper #288*. Many people spend more energy and money on <u>getting good life insurance</u> to help the people they love.

BOOK IS SHORT, HAS FORMS TO QUICKLY SEE, AND USES EMPHASIS

This book is short and may read rough but can be read fast. Long books often lead to misunderstanding of the basics and skimming. This book has legal forms people can quickly see. For emphasis paragraph titles, underlining, and boxes are used. This book capitalizes some legal words like Will, Testator, and Agent but this is optional. To save space some small words are skipped and end quote marks put before punctuation.

THIS BOOK COVERS MAIN LEGAL IDEAS AND SHOULD SUIT MOST PEOPLE

This book covers the main U.S. legal ideas on Estate Planning and major ways New York law is different. This book can't cover all legal issues but should suit most people without strange situations or wishes. <u>Strange situations or wishes that may need research or a lawyer include</u>: a) strange gift wishes for property and money, b) wealth over $5 million, c) big medical concerns like extreme age, d) property or money going to a person with a disability or special needs, and e) wish to move or hide assets to qualify for government help.

LEGAL FORMS CAN HELP MANY AND THIS BOOK HAS STANDARD FORMS

Legal forms are good at most things involved in Estate Planning and can make binding legal documents. Instead of legal forms a lawyer can be used for Estate Planning but it can be costly, take months of work, and they can make mistakes. In life people often pick a cheaper option. Importantly, often a hospital, charity, state agency, or state legislature <u>has written a form most people use and call the "standard form"</u>, and doctors, judges, and other people may not like to follow anything else. This book does provide mostly standard forms.

LEGAL DOCUMENTS MAY NEED TO BE WITNESSED OR NOTARIZED

To be legally enforceable certain legal documents need to be "witnessed", which is someone watching the person doing the form sign and then the witness signs too. Some documents to be enforceable need to be "notarized" which means a person who is a "notary" sees it signed and then uses an ink stamp and signs. Notaries (also called a "notary public") are at some banks, brokers, insurance agents, courts, law offices, libraries, and mailing-copying centers. Using a phonebook to call to find a notary willing to help is common. The words "subscribe" and "execute" means a person signed a document, and "acknowledgment" means a person said a signature was theirs. If a person signs a document in a foreign language it is usually binding. When filling in a form it may help people to know "respectively" in a form means "in the order just stated". When filling out a legal form except for signatures the other parts can be filled in by a person not signing the form, and using pencil is even fine for most parts. Once done often people try to keep the original document and hand out copies. People can have everyone sign many copies to have many copies with ink signatures.

SOME LESS COMMON OR LESS USEFUL FORMS ARE NOT IN THIS BOOK

This book skips some possible but less common or less useful legal documents.

- A "Codicil" can modify a Will but it is easier and legally safer to just rewrite the whole Will.
- Some people do a "Pet Trust" to help a pet, but it's easier to just give money in Will to person given a pet.
- Some people do a "Revocable Living Trust" so a Trust entity with a Trustee holds property or money during their life, usually done to after death have faster transfer of things and avoid small delays, costs, or work of others (by "avoiding probate"). But this is rarely done as it may require moving most of a person's things to a Trust causing maybe years of hassle, mostly to avoid later small work for people happy to be getting things.
- "Childrens Trust" papers can be done (like as part of a Will) so at a death a Trust gets money or property for a minor child to manage until 18, but this is uncommon due to possible cost and hassle, since it rarely matters (as this book explains), and since most Wills already arrange other legal help for young children.
- Though separate forms exist usually organ donation in handled in drivers license or state ID paperwork.
- New York unlike some states does <u>not</u> let a gift list or memo be done after a Will to add more gifts to it.

NO FEDERAL, NEW YORK, OR OTHER TAX IS USUALLY OWED AT A DEATH

Usually no tax is owed as a result of a death, including estate, inheritance, or death taxes.

The Federal Estate And Gift Tax is the only Federal tax that may be owed due to a death, and it only starts when a tax credit is used up that covers $13.61 million a person in 2024 and later.

New York has an estate tax that applies if the dead person died with over $6,940,000 in 2024 and later, and over this amount the tax owed starts at just 3.06% and slowly goes to 16%. Few people die rich enough to owe this tax. No other New York state, county, or city taxes apply if someone dies.

For property or money in another state most states either have no inheritance or estate tax or, alternatively, have a tax credit that covers over $3,000,000 of things, so owing such taxes is rare.

A person's family or Executor may have to file <u>normal</u> income tax returns to cover the partial year a decedent lived and earned income in before they died. Life insurance payouts are usually tax free.

CHAPTER 2
TERMS, PROPERTY LAW, AND HELPFUL INFORMATION FORM

THERE ARE BASIC TERMS AND IDEAS IN ESTATE PLANNING

Some legal terms and ideas are basic to Estate Planning.

■ "Estate Planning" is about people doing legal documents to control things if later absent, sick, or dead. After a document is done people are still mostly free to transfer property, instruct doctors, or change forms.

■ A "person doing a legal document" and "doing a form" means the form is for and affects that person.

■ "Probate" is a legal process to do things after someone's death like transfer property, handle creditors, and authorize a Guardian. Due to changes in the law probate is now often informal, faster, and less costly.

■ A "Will" or "will" (this book uses upper case "W") is a legal document done to control issues after death. The phrase "Last Will And Testament" is used since a "Testament" long ago was a small document done along with a Will to do some things.

■ An "Executor" is a person named in a Will to do things after someone's death. If no Will names someone a judge names an "Administrator" to do this. "Personal Representative" is a blanket term for both these 2.

■ <u>A person doing a Will is called the "Testator"</u> or "Will maker". Before about 1995 a woman Testator was often called a "Testatrix" and woman Executor called an "Executrix" but this is no longer often said or written.

■ If no valid Will is done a person is "intestate" and then a dead person's property and money is transferred to a spouse, children, and family as intestate law says. <u>Some people a fine with this</u>. This is covered later.

■ A person who died is called the "decedent" or "deceased". A person getting a Will gift is called a "recipient", "beneficiary", or "heir" if related (they "inherit"). "Survive" or "surviving" is to be alive after someone else died. The term "descendants" or "issue" usually means a person's children and grandchildren.

■ Legally property is: 1) "real property" which is land and buildings ("real estate"), 2) "fixtures" which are things tied to real property (like fences, carpets, and wired-in appliances), or 3) "personal property" which is everything else (like household items, clothes, tools, cars, jewelry, art, moneys, accounts, and stocks),

■ A person under 18 is usually called a "minor" and often a parent or guardian helps them do things. A minor or other person not reasonably able to make wise decisions lacks "capacity" and is "incapacitated".

■ A document giving power to someone is often called a "Power of Attorney" where the "Principal" gives power to someone called the "Agent" or "Attorney-in-Fact" (but they need not be an actual attorney).

■ State law is the Consolidated Laws of New York, which has parts with different names. Each law is called a "statute" or "section" shown by a "§" or "s" mark. An example of one way to cite a state law is: "N.Y. Surrogate's Court Procedure Act § 101.". A form written in state law for people to find and use if wanted is called a "statutory form". The court that handle most Wills and child issues is Surrogate's Court.

ESTATE MEANS PROPERTY OF DECEDENT AND ENTITY HOLDING THINGS
The "estate" or "probate estate" means all property and money of a dead person that at death or soon after didn't automatically legally go to new owners. Estate is also the name for a temporary entity run by an Executor to do things after a death (it's like a small corporation, e.g., "Estate of John Alan Smith").

PERSON CAN ONLY GIFT IN WILL WHAT THEY OWN AT DEATH
A person can only gift by Will things they own at death, so people should research what they do own. Basically by law a person usually owns all they earn as wages and salary, owns their share of income and profit tied to property they own, and owns or partly owns any things their money buys or improves. And for property with "title" documents (real estate or vehicles) or where there is a "listed owner" (like accounts) the named persons are usually the legal owners unless evidence shows special circumstances. Note, a person during life can sell property, make gifts, or transfer things even if they are named in a Will, so people should consider if they already sold or gave away property they also name in a Will gift.

THINGS OWNED IN SPECIAL WAYS MAY LIMIT GIFTING IN WILL
A person should consider if they own real estate or other property in special ownership ways which may limit gifting by Will. Laws vary in different states but some common special ways of ownership are:
- "joint tenant with right of survivorship" or similar legal options is used in papers, so at a death property goes automatically to other named owners despite what a Will says (this in often how spouses hold a home);
- papers say a "life estate" exists, so then if life of someone ends the other people in papers get item; and
- "Trust property" occurs if paperwork made a Trust entity and then property was transferred into it or this is set to occur, so then the Trust papers control where things put in the Trust go after someone's death.

Simple "joint ownership" with many owners can occur if people do joint papers, all agree to it, buy with joint funds, or if a gift was to many people. Wills can gift joint property, like "I give my half of boat to Ed Hu".

NON-PROBATE TRANSFERS THAT HAPPEN AUTOMATICALLY IGNORE A WILL
It is vital to be aware some money or property of a decedent may automatically transfer on death or soon after to new owners if certain arrangements were made earlier. This is usually called "non-probate property". Such things transfer as arranged even if a Will names the same items in Will gifts.

Examples are: a) a "designated beneficiary" form was done to name people to get an investment or account, b) transfer-on-death accounts were used, and c) real property is held by 2 people as "joint tenants with survivorship" or similar so at a death the surviving person gets things. Also, usually property in a Trust will ignore a Will and transfer as paperwork says to. Life insurance usually goes to the named beneficiary.

Trying to do non-probate transfers for all things is called "avoiding probate", but few people try this since it can cause years of hassle, benefits are small, and often something is missed. When doing a Will people should consider non-probate transfers that will occur automatically at a death and consider what will be left.

HELPFUL INFORMATION FORM CAN HELP TELL FAMILY AND FRIENDS THINGS
People can do an unofficial "Helpful Information" form banks, lawyers, and planners suggest so family or friends after a death will know things. People can staple records or lists to this. See form on next pages.

ESTATE PLANNING HELPFUL INFORMATION

For more space attach copies of form or blank pages. Keep pages by Will or other place for Executor or family.

1. Personal Information (Name, Birthdate, Social Security number, special family details, other):

2. Real estate, vehicles, and other major tangible property (especially if people may not find them):

3. Non-tangible assets like stocks, accounts, investments, loans owed you, and business interests:

4. Possible income or insurance like pensions, retirement, disability, insurance, or contracts:

5. Debts owed by you like credit card, loan, student loan, mortgage, car loans, and accounts payable:

6. Names and information of professionals used (attorneys, accountants, brokers, doctors, others):

7. Computer passwords and helpful files, document places, and safes or safe-deposit boxes code/key:

8. Other helpful things, wishes for funeral, special requests, and last messages to family and friends:

CHAPTER 3
WILL BASICS

WILL LETS A PERSON CONTROL THINGS AFTER THEIR DEATH

A Will is a legal document done by a person to control some things after their death. A person doing a Will is called the "Testator" or "Will maker". In New York a Testator <u>when signing</u> must be at least age 18, of sound mind (rational with sufficient memory), and not be under duress (unfair pressure or threat).

A WILL USUALLY MUST BE SIGNED WITH 2 WITNESSES

WILL MUST SHOW IT'S A WILL AND USUALLY BE SIGNED WITH 2 WITNESSES

In New York a document to be a Will <u>must show it is a Will by its words</u>, and the person doing it usually must <u>sign at the end in front of 2 persons</u> acting as witnesses who then sign too. A Will just spoken on a video or audio recording usually has no legal effect. New York unlike some states doesn't let witnesses be skipped if a Will is handwritten. <u>Some people modify a Will to have 3 or 4 witnesses to help with things later</u>.

WITNESSES SHOULD AT LEAST AGE 18 AND OFTEN NOT GETTING WILL GIFTS

A person to witness a Will must be at least age 18. It is best but not legally required a witness not be very old, live far away, or be named in a Will to be Executor, Guardian, or similar. Usually lawyers try to pick persons to be witnesses who are "disinterested", which means they are not named to get things in a Will. A Will is valid even if 1 or both witnesses are benefiting from a Will (so are not disinterested), but the Will gifts or other benefits to the witness later usually are legally void and not carried out unless there are 2 other disinterested witnesses not benefitting from a Will. See N.Y. Estate, Powers & Trusts Law § 3-3.2. A small exception says a witness if close family can still get up to the amount they'd get by law as close family if there weren't a valid Will. Often people used as witnesses are friends, neighbors, strangers, and family.

TESTATOR SIGNS WILL AND THEN WITNESSES SIGN

A person doing a Will usually signs it with at least 2 witnesses who also sign while all are in 1 room and see others sign. Witnesses usually sign within minutes of Testator and by law it must be within 30 days. People showing others ID is not required but is common. Testator need not initial Will pages though some people do this. A Testator or witness usually <u>use their full legal name</u> unless they dislike and rarely use it. Witnesses only read the 1 paragraph they sign. New York law has witnesses write their "residence address".

TESTATOR MUST DECLARE IT IS THEIR WILL TO THE WITNESSES

<u>In New York a Testator must explain it is a Will to persons who are acting as witnesses</u>. The law says, "The testator shall, at some time during the ceremony or ceremonies of execution and attestation, declare to each of the attesting witnesses that the instrument to which his signature has been affixed is his will". Some lawyers call this "publishing" a Will. Often a Testator doing a Will tells the witnesses a thing like, "My name is ____ this is my Will that I do voluntarily and ask you 2 people to witness". Some Testators also chat a few minutes more about a Will with witnesses to help show they understand what they are doing.

KEEP SIGNED WILL IN SAFE PLACE IT CAN BE FOUND AFTER A DEATH

A Will should be kept so it can be found within days of a death, like in a desk, drawer, safe, with a person, or less often a safe deposit box. It may help to tell family how to get a Will. Also, though rarely done the law lets people during life file a Will in a Surrogate's Court vault and then after death family can go get it. See N.Y. Surrogate's Court Procedure Act § 2507, Reception of wills for safekeeping. If people re-do a Will after filing in a vault they usually remove the old Will from the vault though this is not required.

OFTEN AT START OF A WILL A PERSON NAMES ANY SPOUSE AND CHILDREN

Many Wills start with a place for a Testator to name any current living spouse and children of any age. Natural or adopted children should be put here including any born outside marriage. People without this family can skip this or put "none". Not doing this may invalidate a Will by indicating a person lacks sufficient mental ability, or let a spouse or child not listed ask a judge to give them a share or all of the estate by claiming a Testator just forgot them. After listing family in a Will a Testator is often free to give them nothing.

A WILL NAMES AN EXECUTOR TO DO THINGS AFTER DEATH

A WILL NAMES SOMEONE TO BE EXECUTOR TO DO THINGS AFTER A DEATH

Usually a Will names someone as "Executor" to act after a death. The law gives Executors many helpful legal powers, like to handle debts, find and collect and give new owners property and money, and do probate If a Will fails to name an Executor a judge can pick someone, but family may argue about who to suggest. Note, the term "Personal Representative" and not Executor in recent years is often used for the person doing things after a death, but these terms mostly mean the same thing. Will gifts can go to an Executor.

EXECUTOR CAN BE PAID AND ESTATE PAYS FOR EXECUTOR'S EXPENSES

New York law says a person can ask to can be paid for their work as Executor. New York like some states lets an Executor ask for about 4% of value of the estate (after debts), and this is usually seen as fair. See N.Y. Surrogate's Court Procedure Act § 2307. And reality the Executor often later skips asking for pay to not owe income tax on this pay and to leave more estate resources to carry out Will gifts. Note, expenses an Executor has like for insurance, utilities, repairs, funeral, mortgage, attorneys, and probate costs are paid for with money or property of the estate. A lawyer an Executor hires is paid whatever is agreed on.

EXECUTOR IS PERSON AT LEAST 18 AND SECOND PERSON RARELY NEEDED

In New York a person must be 18 or older to be Executor. Often named in Will is a spouse, adult child, distant family, or friend. A bank or lawyer can be Executor but they charge high fees. A person may not be a criminal felon and a non-resident alien (person not a U.S. citizen) may have to name a local Co-Executor and later talk to the judge. An Executor need not be a New York resident. A judge may later remove or not appoint a person for reasons like if illiteracy or bad character seems a problem. Naming 2 people to both be Executor is allowed but rare due to the risk of legal issues, and since any 1 person named should be trusted. People can name a 2nd person to be Executor if the 1st person isn't later available but most skip this since this rarely occurs and if needed a judge can just pick someone. To add such a 2nd person a person could add:"or if they are reasonably unable or unwilling to serve I name _____ to serve".

CANCELING OLD WILLS IS USUALLY NOT A PROBLEM

So a new Will is followed old Wills should be canceled ("revoked") but this is easy and rarely a problem. A new Will usually quickly says old Wills are revoked to cancel them, and all this book's Will forms say this. Or people can revoke an old Will by writing "void" or "cancelled" or "X" on it, preferably with a witness to this. Usually crossing out just part of a Will has no effect. Revoking a Will usually doesn't bring back an earlier Will.

MOST WILLS HAVE A MISCELLANEOUS PART WITH HELPFUL LANGUAGE

Most Wills have a "Miscellaneous" page with paragraphs of legal language to avoid some legal problems. This can help if later legal problems occur. A person doing a Will need not understand these paragraphs.

MOST WILLS SAY PEOPLE MAY LATER DO INFORMAL PROBATE

Most Wills helpfully say later the family and friends may do "informal probate" which can avoid costs and delays. Informal probate often is done with just 1 court hearing and often is completed in well under 1 year.

MOST WILLS SAY TO SKIP COSTLY BOND FOR EXECUTOR AND OTHERS

Most Wills helpfully say no "bond" or "surety" is required for any Executor, Guardian, or similar person. A bond is insurance from a company to insure against misconduct. A Testator usually doesn't want a bond since the persons Testator names are trusted and them later needing a bond will cost the estate money.

LATER DIVORCE OR MURDER CANCELS WILL GIFTS TO A PERSON

New York law says a person divorcing or murdering a Testator usually cancels Will gifts to the person.

PROBABLY DO NEW DOCUMENTS IF DIVORCE, MARRY, HAVE CHILD, OR MOVE

Divorcing, marrying, having a new child, or moving to a new state can have big legal effects, and if any of these events occur it is recommended people do a new Will and other Estate Planning papers soon. To help most states say a Will from another state is still valid if people move but this is not always certain.

CHAPTER 4
WILL GIFTS INCLUDING RESIDUE CLAUSE

MAIN USE OF A WILL IS TO WRITE GIFTS TO HAPPEN AFTER DEATH

Most people use a Will mainly to legally say what happens to their property and money after their death, usually by writing down various Will gifts to occur when they die. Verbal and even writings about this are not usually valid if not in a written Will. A Will can control property acquired after it was signed. The end of this Chapter covers "intestate law" which says where a person's things go at death if no valid Will handles this.

RESIDUE CLAUSE IS CATCH-ALL THAT HELPFULLY GIFTS ANYTHING LEFT

Most Wills by their end have a Residue Clause to gift property or money not already gifted in a Will or used other ways, often called a "catch-all" or "left-over" clause. This is covered later in this Chapter.

GIFTING IN A WILL USING SIMPLE WORDS OFTEN IS BEST

Making gifts in a Will using simple words is often best, using words like "I give to" and "I gift to". This is legally fine and avoids confusing legal words like "bequest", "devise", and "legacy" which few people know.

A PERSON IS MOSTLY FREE TO GIFT THEIR THINGS AS WANTED

A person is mostly free to give at death their money and property as they want. But creditors a decedent owed money, a spouse, and minor children under age 18 may have some rights which this book later covers.

IN WILL CAN DO SPECIFIC GIFTS TO GIFT PARTICULAR PROPERTY

Most Wills have "specific gifts" to gift <u>particular things</u>. Specific gifts can be any property, like "I give boat to Ed Blom" and "I give UBank account #84553873 to Sue Wu". If a gift is not clear the law assumes all of a kind of thing is given, like "I give jewelry to Ann Po" means <u>all</u> jewelry. But gifting specific property can have surprises like value of items can change, or a Will gift may later fail to occur if property is not owned at death.

IN WILL CAN DO GENERAL GIFTS LIKE OF MONEY

Wills can do "general gifts" where what is gifted is not particular property but can be flexibly chosen, like "I give 1 of my 3 cars to Ed Po" which lets an Executor pick which car. The usual general gift is money, like "I give $5 to Ed Hu". Money gifts are easy to write, let equal gifts be made, and are legally safer for many reasons. To carry out money gifts an Executor usually uses accounts or sells some property in the estate.

PERSON IN WILL GIFT USUALLY MUST SURVIVE OR GIFT DOES NOT OCCUR

Many Wills like this book's Will forms say a person named in a Will gift must survive (live past) the Testator for the gift to occur unless gift language specifically says different. If survival is not required for a Will gift what happens if a named recipient is dead can be unclear (state laws can be very complex). <u>People doing a Will should consider how Will gifts to people dying before Testator usually have no effect</u>. People if they see a person in a Will gift has died can re-do a Will or just let the Residue Clause handle it.

CONDITIONS ON WILL GIFTS ARE RARE DUE TO POSSIBLE PROBLEMS

Putting conditions on a gift, like "I give Ann Poe $90 if she graduates college", can cause problems like years of delay, risk of lawsuits, and big attorney's fees. Due to all this conditions are rarely put on Will gifts.

PROPERTY OR MONEY IN A JOINT GIFT GOES TO MULTIPLE PEOPLE

The same property or money in a "joint gift" can go to many people to each get a part. For example, "I give boat and all hats to Ann Baxter and Mary Ann Swanson" means each person owns part of every item. People later can split things by agreement or an Executor can decide how to divide items. If a person in a joint gift has died their part usually is left to transfer under a Residue Clause.

PEOPLE CAN ADD AN ALTERNATE BENEFICIARY LIKE FOR SPECIAL ITEMS

A person named in a Will gift dying before a Testator is rare, and if seen people can re-do a Will to name new persons or let a Will's Residue Clause handle it. Some people to prepare for this chance maybe for special items write an "alternate beneficiary", like "I give boat to Ed Liu but if they don't survive me to Ann Liu".

CAN SAY IF PERSON IN GIFT DIES THEN IT GOES TO LINEAL DESCENDANTS

A Will gift can say it goes to a person but if they don't survive then to their "lineal descendants per stirpes". Descendants are a person's children and grandchildren. "Per stirpes" means "by branch" and is about how to spread property and money, and it mostly tries to divide things so each family branch gets an equal share. Most Wills use "lineal descendants" language in a Residue Clause. An example shows how it works:

A Will may say: **"Clothes to Sue Wu but if they don't survive to their lineal descendants per stirpes"**, and this means if Sue Wu has died and her son Ken Wu is living and her other son Ben Wu has died but left 2 children then, legally, under the law Ken Wu himself gets 50% and Ben Wu's 2 children each get 25%.

GIFT BENEFICIARIES CAN GET PERCENTAGE RATHER THAN EQUAL SHARE

If a Will gift goes to multiple people the law assumes equal shares, but if wanted percentages can be used to make unequal gifts, like "I give boat 90% to John Smith and 10% to Mary Baker".

GIFTS IN WILL CAN GO TO A GROUP OR CLASS OF PEOPLE

To save work a Will gift can go to a group or class of people like certain family if who is meant is later easy to determine. People can say roughly how much in total is gifted to be clearer. Examples are: "I give $10 to each person on my 2018 soccer team" and "I give $10 to each of my grandkids so this is about $100 in total."

AFTER A DEATH FAMILIES OFTEN LET PEOPLE TAKE ITEMS UNOFFICIALLY

Many families unofficially let people take items in ways a dead person said, showed by stickers, or wrote on a note, which is often fine. If anyone objects a judge often has the Will and law be followed fully but later people can voluntarily retransfer items. Unlike many states New York does not officially let a memo or list written after a Will modify or add new gifts to occur after a person's death (but as just explained many people do these anyway).

RESIDUE CLAUSE GIFTING ALL LEFT IS MAIN WAY USED TO GIFT THINGS

THE RESIDUE CLAUSE IS CATCH-ALL THAT HELPS GIFT ANYTHING LEFT

Most Wills by their end have a Residue Clause to gift any property or money not gifted earlier in a Will or used in other ways. Things transferred this way is called the "Residue". Many people gift most their money and property this way by intentionally not mentioning in a Will most things so the Residue Clause handles it. This avoids need to describe things and has less legal risk. After applying a Residue Clause if anything is somehow left then by law a decedent's closest heirs-at-law get things (this is their closest family).

USUAL RESIDUE CLAUSE HAS 2 PARTS

A short 2 part Residue Clause is usual and is used in this book's Will forms, and it has:

1) 1st space to name 1 or more persons to get things if they survive Testator (many name a spouse or closest family here), and if several people are named but only some survive then survivors split things, and

2) 2nd space to name persons to get things if all in the 1st space don't survive (many people name next close family or friends in this space), and if a person in 2nd space has died their descendants get their share.

EXAMPLE OF 2 PART RESIDUE CLAUSE:

"RESIDUE CLAUSE: I give money and property not gifted earlier, the residue:
   a) to   John Paul Doe my husband   who survive me with persons just named who survive me taking the share of non-survivors, then if anything remains
   b) to   Sam Doe, Beth Wu, and Greta Fisher   and if any of those just named do not survive me their part goes to their lineal descendants per stirpes."

In this example if John Paul Doe has survived he gets all things, but if John Paul Doe hasn't survived and also Sam Doe hasn't survived and he left 2 daughters then those 2 daughters split the 1/3 share of his (so get 1/6 each) and the other 2 persons in the second part Beth Wu and Greta Fisher get 1/3 each.

A FEW PEOPLE REWRITE RESIDUE CLAUSE TO HAVE 1 PART

A normal Residue Clause of 2 parts is often fine for most people. But a few people modify a Will to have a "1 Part Residue Clause" since it tends to gift to a group more equally and be simpler to understand. People with no spouse and no young children are likelier to do this change, but even they often don't bother. See Example below for exact words to use if people want to change to a 1 Part Residue Clause.

EXAMPLE OF 1 PART RESIDUE CLAUSE:

"RESIDUE CLAUSE: The rest, residue, and remainder of my estate, property of any kind and nature, and anything I have an interest in, I give to Adam Doe and Beth Wu   who survive me and to lineal descendants per stirpes of any person just named who did not survive me."

In this example if Adam hasn't survived but had 2 children they each get 25%, and if Beth Wu survived she gets 50%. Or if Beth Wu also hadn't survived and had 5 kids they split her part and each gets 10%.

MUST SUFFICIENTLY DESCRIBE NAMES AND PROPERTY IN A WILL

PUTTING NAMES OF PEOPLE OR GROUPS IN A WILL IS FAIRLY EASY

Putting names in Wills is fairly easy. <u>A judge or Executor assume a person in a Will meant people they know, so common names are OK unless 2 friends or family have the same name</u>. Details can help if names won't be recognized or to be friendly, like "I give $5 to my nurse Sue Ax" and "I give $5 to loyal pal Ed Lee". If people used a nickname "also known as" or "a/k/a" may help, like "I give $5 to Dan Smith a/k/a Old Fishy". Gifts can go to a charity, government, or group, like "I give $10 to YMCA of USA", "I give $80 to Erie County Public Library, New York", and "I give $50 to Wix Church, Rex, TX". People can phone for a charity's name.

PUTTING DESCRIPTIONS OF ITEMS IN WILL GIFTS IS FAIRLY EASY

Describing items in gifts is easy since people rarely own similar items. Often fine are gifts like: "I give ax to Ed Wu" and "I give big table to Ann Fox". It's OK to gift by category or list, like: "I give tools to Sam Lee" and "I give cow, van, and harp to Sue Hill". Financial assets can use plain words, like "bank accounts" or "stocks", but details can help, like: "US Bank account ending #1511". <u>Gifting using a location is riskier</u> as judges will ignore Will gifts if it seems items were placed to affect gifting and no "independently significant" life reason. So, "I give Ed Po items in safe and desk" judges might not follow, but "I give Ed Po hats in attic" likely is OK.

DESCRIBING REAL PROPERTY IS HARD IF NOT USING RESIDUE OR TITLE

The easier, legally safer way to transfer real property (real estate) at death is: 1) do nothing specific so it's handled by a Will Residue Clause, or 2) have a lawyer or agent put names in a deed or similar document so then named persons legally get things at someone's death. Most use these 2 ways to transfer real property.

Gifting real property other ways is harder though possible. Helpfully a Will gift of real property <u>described by location</u> legally does gift <u>all land, buildings, and fixtures located there</u> with no need to describe what's there.

It is possible to <u>gift real property at a particular address with very plain words</u>, like a house, fixtures, and land can be fully given by something like: "I give 81 Maxwell Street, Albany, New York, to Mary Ann Brown".

People can do a <u>blanket gift</u> giving all of a kind of property, like, "I give all real property and fixtures in Kings County, New York to Ann Ivy Hill " or "I give all furniture and all bank accounts to Eric Paul Carlson".

Giving real property in a Will using a "legal description" is how many lawyers do it, but this can be hard to do. If using a legal description people must copy without mistakes <u>the full legal description of maybe many lines</u> into a Will with no abbreviation at all. A legal description might be found on a deed or on mortgage papers. Legal descriptions may refer to a "lot" or "blocks" on a map which is recorded in land records of a county, or it may refer to a path around the land borders with various angles, distances, and iron stakes.

CAN LEAVE SOME WILL GIFT LINES BLANK OR WRITE TO SAY SKIP

A person writing a Will can choose to not use some gifts lines in a Will legal form, like by just leaving them blank, writing things like "SKIPPED" or "NONE" in them, or using a computer to delete some gift lines. Judges and others usually do not care about neatness or empty spaces in Wills.

MOST STATES AND WILLS SAY PEOPLE TO GET GIFTS MUST SURVIVE 5 DAYS

Helpful laws in most states and all this book's Will forms say if a person dies within 5 days (120 hours) or simultaneously with a Testator, then they are legally seen as dying before Testator. This skips the need to prove exact time of death (like if people die in 1 accident), and avoids a Will gift or right to something going to someone who then soon dies within days (so an item may have to go through multiple probate proceedings).

INTESTATE LAW COVERS PROPERTY OR MONEY NOT HANDLED BY WILL

INTESTATE LAW CONTROLS THINGS NOT HANDLED BY A WILL OR SIMILAR

State "intestate" law at N.Y. Estates, Powers & Trusts Law § 4-1.1 says <u>if a person dies with no valid Will</u> or <u>if anything is left after Will and transfers are done</u> then certain surviving (living) family get that money and property. "Intestate" means to not have a Will. Many people like how intestate law transfers things and choose to skip a Will, but often doing a Will has some other benefits. <u>Note, the term "descendants" means a person's children and grandchildren</u>, and if someone has died who would have got an intestate share often their descendants under intestate law get that share. New York intestate law if it applies says, in order:

1) if decedent (the person who died) left some surviving (living) descendants but no surviving spouse, then the descendants get all of the property and money in the decedent's estate;

2) if decedent left a surviving spouse and no descendants, then the spouse gets all the estate;

3) if decedent left a surviving spouse and also descendants, then the spouse gets the first $50,000 of things of value and 1/2 the rest, and the descendants split the remainder;

4) if decedent left no surviving spouse or descendants then things go to decedent's next nearest relatives starting with decedent's parents, then brothers and sisters, then cousins, and then other close family; and

5) if none of the above persons survive, then the decedent's estate goes to the state of New York.

SIMPLE WILL WITH MOST GIFTING DONE BY RESIDUE CLAUSE OFTEN IS BEST

<u>Writing a simple Will without many gifts, much left blank, and mostly using a Residue Clause is often best</u>.

If there is <u>no spouse and no children</u> often a person does a few small gifts, and then names some family or friends in the Residue Clause to get everything remaining.

If there <u>is only a spouse</u> often a person does small gifts to friends and family, then uses the Residue Clause of the Will to gift all left to the spouse, and then names a few fallback persons in the Residue Clause.

<u>A parent with young children if married to the other parent</u> often does small gifts to friends and family, then in the Residue Clause gives mostly to a spouse, and then names children as fallbacks in the Residue Clause.

<u>A parent with young children if not married or close to the other parent</u> often does small gifts to friends and family, and then uses the Residue Clause to gift all remaining to the children.

CHAPTER 5
DEBT, MARRIAGE, AND YOUNG CHILD ISSUES

THIS CHAPTER COVERS CERTAIN ISSUES THAT SOME PEOPLE CAN SKIP
This Chapter covers debt, marriage, and young child issues, and some people can skip parts of this.

DEBT ISSUES

PAYING DECEDENT'S DEBTS MAY USE UP RESOURCES AND REDUCE GIFTS
If a decedent had debts then creditors may ask a judge to be paid from decedent's money or property before Will gifts and certain transfers occur. How debts are paid is set by state law and a Will need not describe this. Money to pay debts comes from decedent's money and property so may affect (in order) the Will Residue, Will general gifts, Will specific gifts, and non-probate transfers. Health care, taxes, probate, and funeral costs by law have some priority to be paid first. For various reasons often not all debts are paid. People should consider how paying debts may use up money or property, leaving less to carry out Will gifts. A spouse and family usually aren't liable for decedent's debts unless they actually guaranteed or co-signed.

SECURED DEBTS LIKE MORTGAGE OR VEHICLE LIEN ARE NOT PAID OFF
Laws in most states say do not pay off secured debts on property of a decedent like a house mortgage or vehicle lien even if other debts are paid by Executor or in probate. This avoids using up estate resources on paying these usually big debts and leaves more estate resources to carry out Will gifts and other transfers. Due to this, all this book's Will forms say do not usually pay off any secured debts. But if a Testator wants they can 1) put in a Will an order to pay (like, "Executor pay off the house mortgage"), or 2) gift enough money to pay off a secured debt to the person getting the property. Most banks let the new owners after a death keep paying monthly any secured debt like a mortgage or lien.

FAMILY RIGHTS MAY BE USED TO GET FAMILY THINGS BEFORE DEBTS
Most states have "Family Rights" a decedent's surviving spouse or children can claim, and this helpfully may let them get things even before most debts of decedent are paid and even before Will gifts.

First, in many states a surviving spouse (or if there is no spouse then decedent's younger children) can use an "Exempt Property" right to get ownership of some of a decedent's household items, vehicles, and other things to use to live. New York law in particular says a spouse (or if there's no spouse then children to age 21) can claim from decedent's things a) $25,000 of household items (but not if used in a business), b) 1 car worth up to $25,000 (or cash equal to this), c) cash including from accounts of $25,000, d) books, photos, and other media worth $2500, and e) domestic or farm animals and farm equipment of up to $20,000. See N.Y. Estates, Powers & Trusts Law § 5-3.1. Family can even try to keep more things by saying decedent verbally gave them items.

Second, in many states a surviving spouse and young children can use a "Family Allowance" right to get some of a decedent's money and property to live on for 1 year or so. New York is unusual and does not have any allowance to help support a spouse or family. New York does have a "Small Estate Affidavit" which for small estates with under $50,000 of things may let family claim most of what there is quickly.

Third, in many states a surviving spouse or young children have some right to get (or stay in for years) the house or mobile home owned by a decedent under a "Homestead Law". New York is unusual and does not have this. But people in New York often put a spouse or child on the land title as a "joint tenant" or similar so they get ownership of a house automatically. New York law does say creditors trying to collect what decedent owed who are without a mortgage usually can't bother a house going to family. No matter what a spouse or children living in a home may be legally and practically very hard to remove. So family don't try to cause legal trouble about a house usually a person gives a house mostly to a spouse or young children.

MARRIAGE ISSUES

NEW YORK USES SEPARATE PROPERTY LAW FOR SPOUSES

New York like most states uses the Separate Property Law system that says a married person mostly owns their money and property separately and not jointly with a spouse. Due to this a married person is largely free to sell during life or gift by Will most of their money or property and not have to involve a spouse. But joint ownership by 2 spouses and not separate ownership can arise in other ways, like by agreement, both spouses paying part of the purchase price, if a gift was to both spouses, or if paperwork calls it joint.

COMMUNITY PROPERTY LAW APPLIES IN OTHER STATES FOR SPOUSES

There are 9 states mostly in the Western U.S. that use the Community Property Law system for spouses (Arizona, California, Louisiana, Idaho, Nevada, New Mexico, Texas, Washington, and Wisconsin). This says property or money is owned 50/50 by spouses as Community Property if it's from mental or physical work while married (like wages or salary) or if items are bought or improved with any other Community Property. Married people very recently moving from these states may face legal issues.

JOINT WILL OR SIMILAR BOTH SPOUSES SIGN IS NOT RECOMMENDED

Some couples who worry a lot try to sign a "Joint Will" or a "Contract To Make A Will" done by a lawyer which says spouses give all to the other if they die first, then says last living spouse gives to all children equally, and usually says a spouse may not change this. This is banned in some states and is rarely used.

SPOUSE CAN CLAIM ELECTIVE SHARE INSTEAD OF THEM FOLLOWING WILL

A spouse if unhappy with what a Will and other transfers may give them has a right to instead choose (elect) an "Elective Share" of a share of decedent's property and money rather than take what a Will says. State laws do this for fairness, so a spouse has resources to live on, and so early divorce isn't the only way to be financially secure. To avoid this spouses can sign a pre-nuptial or a post-nuptial agreement written by a lawyer but this can be costly to do. New York law says the Elective Share is 1/3 of the decedent's money and property with some modifications, or if decedent didn't leave much then all of the first $50,000 of things. Clearly if a spouse chooses to use an Elective Share to get 1/3 or so of a decedent's money and property this may use up so much it interferes with other transfers. To avoid a spouse wanting to use the Elective Share most people give over 1/2 of their things to any spouse of theirs.

YOUNG CHILD ISSUES

WILL CAN NAME A GUARDIAN OF THE PERSON TO CARE FOR YOUNG CHILD

If a parent dies with a child under age 18 then any other natural or adopted parent (but not a step-parent) almost always automatically gets control of the child's care (including health care, school, and home issues). This won't occur only if the other parent will be unavailable a long time or is proven unfit in court which is rare. But just in case it is later needed (like later both parents of a child die) a Will often names a healthy and willing relative or friend as "Guardian of the Person" to give this care for a young child.

WILL CAN NAME A GUARDIAN OF PROPERTY TO MANAGE CHILD'S PROPERTY

Since a child until age 18 can't legally easily control property including money a Will often names a person to be "Guardian of Property" of a minor to have the job of managing a young child's property and money. New York also calls this a "Guardian for Infant's Property". Many states call this a "Guardian of the Estate" or "Conservator". This person says each month how to use property and money on a child's needs (like on school, living, and health care) and then usually at age 18 any money and property left is handed to the child. Any person paying things for a child can ask to be paid back. Judges may hold a yearly hearing on spending. As a nice 2nd option to avoid work and costs most Wills say an Executor may name a person (including themselves) as "Custodian" to manage things using the new helpful Uniform Transfers To Minors Act.

MOST WILLS NAME 1 PERSON TO CARE FOR CHILD AND THEIR PROPERTY

Most parents and this book's Will forms name the same 1 person to care for a child and also manage a child's property and money. People can change a Will to name different people for the 2 positions, but this is rarely worth it since parents dying is rare, rarely do children get much, a person smart enough to handle a child often can handle money, and naming different people can lead to arguments and even costly lawsuits between people. Will gifts can go to someone named to be a Guardian.

PERSON TO HELP A CHILD MUST BE AT LEAST 18

To be a Guardian of any kind for a minor in New York a person must be at least age 18 but they needn't live here. Later usually a judge can't think a person is unfit to serve as Guardian, which usually means they have no history of criminal felonies, abuse, or fraud. The choice made by the last living parent is usually followed. If no Will names a person for a position or they're unavailable a judge can pick someone, but family may argue about who to suggest. Naming 2 people to act at the same time in the same position is rare since 2 persons may argue and any 1 person named should be smart enough to act alone. In rare cases a married couple is named for the same position but there can be problems if they divorce or disagree. Importantly, some Wills add a 2nd person to serve if the 1st person named is later not available, like by adding: "or if they are later unable to serve I name _____ to serve"). But most people skip naming a fallback person since it is rarely needed, if a problem is seen a Will can be redone by a person, and a judge can just pick someone if needed.

NAMING PERSONS TO HELP CHILD RARELY MATTERS

A child under 18 having parents die is rare so parents shouldn't worry much about naming people to help. A good U.S. study looked at 72,240 people under age 18 and found only 2014 had lost 1 parent (so 2.78%) and only 97 had lost 2 parents (so a very small 0.13%). *Parent Mortality Census SIPP Paper #288.*

CHAPTER 6
BASIC IDEAS ABOUT HEALTH CARE FORMS

BASIC IDEAS HELP PEOPLE UNDERSTAND CONTROLLING HEALTH CARE

Some ideas help people understand health care forms.

■ By law people control their own health care by telling doctors and others what they want <u>unless they're "incapacitated"</u> by insufficient ability to a) <u>communicate</u> verbally or by notes, b) be <u>rational</u>, or c) be <u>conscious</u>. In actuality most people keep control of their own health care till death or till no big treatment options remain, but people may worry they may be incapacitated a long time so they want to do health care forms.

■ If an adult 18 or older becomes incapacitated <u>the adult's closest family like spouse or adult child can make emergency decisions</u> but they usually must then rush to a judge to get further power if no legal document gives them full power over health care.

■ In forms a <u>person can be named to have control of health care</u> if needed who is often called "Agent". Forms about control of health care if people are later incapacitated are often called "Advanced Directives".

■ In forms people can give <u>written health care instructions that doctors, family, and Agent must obey</u>.

■ Parents do have power over health care of <u>their children under age 18</u>.

■ Some <u>young married people</u> give a spouse power over health care in case they are ever incapacitated. Some <u>young adults</u> give this power to parents. Young people are less often ill so often skip doing things.

■ Pain relief like pain drugs and comfort care is usually given even if forms say to stop or limit other care.

■ <u>Most people only do a single long health care form</u> that has a spot to give someone power over health care and a spot for instructions (this is often called a "Health Care Power of Attorney" though names vary).

■ For the rare cases when saying to stop health care likely matters due to extreme illness or old age:

-- most people do nothing special and trust family or Agent for health care to decide on stopping care based on many factors like pain, cost, hassle, suffering and time of treatment, beliefs, and chances of recovery;

-- a few people do a serious document to say to stop most health care if <u>later</u> doctors decide a person is incapacitated, is in bad medical condition (irrevocable terminal condition or unlikely to regain consciousness), and more medical care won't help (this document to stop care is often called a "Living Will" but names vary);

-- a few people do a serious document to <u>starting immediately</u> block certain health care (and this often is called a "Do-Not-Resuscitate" if about resuscitation or called a "Physician's Order" if about many treatments).

CHAPTER 7
FORM 1: WILL (STANDARD)

FORM 1 IS A STANDARD WILL THAT IS FLEXIBLE BUT WITHOUT A GUARDIAN

Form 1 is a flexible Will that lets a person control many things after their death. This form has no part about a Guardian so is for someone with no child under age 18. A person doing a Will is called a Testator.

THIS FORM IS A WILL WITH SEVERAL PARTS

The form starts with lines for a person to put their name (a full legal name is best but not required) and place of main residence (most put a county but some put a city). The Will is still valid if people later move.

Paragraph 1, "List Of Spouse And Children", lets a person write the names of any living spouse and children they have, or if none maybe write "none". This helps show a person has enough mental ability and memory to do a Will. Not listing a living spouse or child here can let an omitted person ask a judge to give them a share or all of a Testator's property and money by claiming they were accidentally forgotten.

Paragraph 2, "Gifts", has many spaces to make either specific gifts of particular property or general gifts like of money. People can delete, copy and paste to add more, or leave blank these gift lines.

Paragraph 3, "Residue", has a Residue Clause to say any property and money left after other Will parts and other transfers is to be distributed in the way a person wrote in the blank parts of this paragraph.

Paragraph 4, "Administration", names a person to be Personal Representative to do things after a person's death (in the past the similar term Executor was used in New York for the person doing this).

Paragraph 5, "Miscellaneous", has paragraphs of legal language to help avoid certain legal issues.

Last is a paragraph for the person doing the Will as Testator to put the date and sign, and also a paragraph for 2 witnesses to put the date, sign, and print the addresses they live at.

USUAL RESIDUE CLAUSE HAS 2 PLACES TO NAME PERSONS TO GET THINGS

In a Will "Residue Clause" anything left over after other Will parts is transferred as the clause directs. Many people use a Residue Clause to gift most their things. In this Will form's Residue Clause there is:

1) a 1st space to name 1 or more persons to get the Residue, and if any named here have died before the Will maker then other persons named here in this 1st space take the dead person's share, and

2) a 2nd space to name people to get things if all people named in the 1st space have died, and if any people named in the 2nd space have died their shares go to "lineal descendants" like their children.

People often put in the 1st space a spouse or closest family or friends, and in 2nd space next closest people.

TESTATOR AND 2 WITNESSES WHILE TOGETHER SIGN WILL

This Will after being filled out (except bits intentionally left blank) must be signed by the person doing the Will (as the Testator) in front of at least 2 persons acting as witnesses at least age 18 who then also sign. Under New York law the Testator doing the Will must also verbally tell witnesses the document is their Will.

LAST WILL AND TESTAMENT

I, _____, of _____, New York do revoke all prior Wills and testamentary documents and do make, publish, and declare this as my Will. I am of sound mind and under no duress or undue influence and acting voluntarily.

1. LIST OF SPOUSE AND CHILDREN. To help show I am mentally competent and have sufficient memory to make a Will I wish to list any living spouse and living children I now have. I currently have the following living spouse and living children:
_____
_____.

2. GIFTS. I give these gifts in this Will, but to get a gift in this section the recipient must survive me except as otherwise stated below.

I give _____ to _____.

I give _____ to _____.

I give _____ to _____.

I give _____ to _____.

I give _____ to _____.

I give _____ to _____.

I give _____ to _____.

I give _____ to _____.

I give _____ to _____.

I give _____ to _____.

3. RESIDUE. I give the rest and residue and remainder of my estate, my money and property of any kind and nature, and anything I have an interest in so long as it was not transferred by other Will provisions, as follows:
  a) to _____ who survive me with persons just named who survive me taking the share of non-survivors, then if anything remains
  b) to _____ and if any of those just named do not survive me their part goes to their lineal descendants per stirpes.

4. ADMINISTRATION. I name, nominate, and appoint _____
as Executor including for me, my Will, and my estate.

5. MISCELLANEOUS. The following applies to this Will and generally.
    In this Will no part left unfilled is a mistake including spaces in the residue clause.
    The facts support and I want New York state law to apply to this Will and my estate.
    If context allows in this Will or other documents the terms Executor and Administrator and Personal Representative are interchangeable. If context allows Conservator and Guardian of Property and Guardian of the Estate and Conservator and Custodian are interchangeable. Any such person has all powers and rights of the others.
    I order that my just debts, funeral and related expenses, and taxes be paid as soon after my death as practical but only those items my Executor chooses to pay.
    Priority of Will gifts of the same type is based on the order they are written.
    The words "give" and "gift" also means a devise, bequest, grant, legacy, or similar.
    I am intentionally not providing by Will or other ways for some family, including I am not providing for some children of mine and also children of a deceased child of mine.
    If a gift Will reasonably mentions survival then survival is an absolute condition and anti-lapse laws or similar provisions have no effect and without survival the gift lapses. Unless a Will gift specifies otherwise if a Will gift goes to multiple recipients if any do not survive me the part to them lapses and instead goes to other surviving recipients.
    No earlier transfer reduces a Will gift unless I usually called it a loan or advancement.
    In this Will any gender or gendered word includes all genders, and the singular includes the plural and vice versa, and "they" can mean a single person or many persons.
    Unless a Will specifically says otherwise a secured debt including a mortgage or lien shall not be paid off including by Executor or in probate, and a recipient of a Will gift of property takes it subject to debts. Also, no recipient of property who may lose it or who pays to keep it may have my estate or others pay or do exoneration.
    If during my life I disposed of an item in a specific gift then the gift is extinguished (including ademption shall apply and it shall adeem).
    I request and authorize any informal, summary, and quick probate or similar action. Any Executor may act independently with no supervision of any court, including independent administration, and with no inventory, appraisal, or other action.
    Any Guardian of any type, Conservator, Custodian, or other person managing a minor's property or money may use or invade the principal and sell property without court action.
    I give any Executor the a) fullest authority, discretion, and powers allowed by state law, b) power to lease, sell, mortgage, convey, or keep property including real property in a manner and time they deem helpful or proper, and c) authority to settle or pay claims or debts in the time and manner they choose. Any Executor also shall have and possess all powers and authorities conferred by statute or common law in any jurisdiction where Executor may act, including those from the New York Estates Powers & Trusts Law as

amended, except for instances which conflict with the express provisions of this Will.

The residue includes lapsed or failed gifts, insurance paid to the estate, digital assets, inheritances owed me, and all I had power of appointment or testamentary disposition over.

Any Executor may access, manage, delete, modify, transfer, and otherwise control any digital accounts and assets I had any interest in or power over.

Any Executor, Personal Representative, Administrator, Guardian of any type like for a person or estate, Conservator, Custodian, and any other fiduciary under this Will or otherwise shall qualify and serve without bond, surety, security, surety bond, or similar.

If evidence does not show it likely a person survived me by 120 hours (5 days) then for this Will and my estate they shall be deemed in all ways as having died before me.

If part of this Will is by law invalid or unenforceable other provisions remain in effect.

Any Executor may at any time transfer money or property of a minor under age 18 to a Custodian to serve under the New York Uniform Transfers to Minors Act or similar law anywhere, and may pick a person to be Custodian including themselves.

TESTATOR

IN WITNESS WHEREOF, I, _____, the Testator, declare I have signed this Will which I do and make voluntarily, on the ____ day of _____, 20____.

_____
Signature of Testator

WITNESSES

The foregoing instrument was signed by the Testator in our presence and declared by the Testator to be the Testator's Will, and we, the Witnesses who sign below, sign our names hereunto to act as witnesses at the request and in the presence of the Testator, and in the presence of each other on the ____ day of _____, 20____.

_____   _____
Signature of Witness #1   Residence Address of Witness #1

_____   _____
Signature of Witness #2   Residence Address of Witness #2

CHAPTER 8
FORM 2: WILL (GUARDIAN)

FORM 2 IS A WILL WITH GUARDIAN PART FOR PERSON WITH YOUNG CHILD

Form 2 is a Will with a Guardian part to be used by a person with a minor child under the age of 18. A person doing a Will is called a Testator.

FORM IS A WILL WITH SEVERAL PARTS INCLUDING A GUARDIAN PART

The form starts with lines for a person to put their name (a full legal name is best but not required) and place of main residence (most put a county but some put a city). The Will is still valid if people later move.

Paragraph 1, "List Of Spouse And Children", lets a person write the names of any living spouse and children they have, or if none maybe write "none". This helps show a Testator has enough mental ability and memory to do a Will. Not listing a living spouse or child here can let an omitted person ask a judge to give them a share or all of a Testator's property and money by claiming they were accidently forgotten.

Paragraph 2, "Gifts", has many spaces to make either specific gifts of particular property or general gifts like of money. People can delete, copy and paste to add more, or leave blank these gift lines.

Paragraph 3, "Residue", has a Residue Clause to say any property and money left after other Will parts and other transfers is to be distributed in the way a person wrote in the blank parts of this paragraph.

Paragraph 4, "Administration", names a person to be Executor to do things after a person's death (some people especially in other states use the term "Personal Representative" for this).

<u>**Paragraph 5, "Guardian"**, names a person as Guardian of the Person to care for minor children under 18 if needed (like if both parents die) and Guardian of the Property to manage property and money of a child.</u>

Paragraph 6, "Miscellaneous", has paragraphs of legal language to help avoid certain legal issues.

Last is a paragraph for the person doing the Will as Testator to put the date and sign, and also a paragraph for 2 witnesses to put the date, sign, and print the addresses they live at.

USUAL RESIDUE CLAUSE HAS 2 PLACES TO NAME PERSONS TO GET THINGS

In a Will "Residue Clause" anything left over after other Will parts is transferred as the clause directs. Many people use a Residue Clause to gift most their things. In this Will form's Residue Clause there is:

1) a 1st space to name 1 or more persons to get the Residue, and if any named here have died before the Will maker then other persons named here in this 1st space take the dead person's share, and

2) a 2nd space to name people to get things if all people named in the 1st space have died, and if any people named in the 2nd space have died their shares go to "lineal descendants" like their children.

People often put in the 1st space a spouse or closest family or friends, and in 2nd space next closest people.

TESTATOR AND 2 WITNESSES WHILE TOGETHER SIGN WILL

This Will after being filled out (except bits intentionally left blank) must be signed by the person doing the Will (as the Testator) in front of at least 2 persons acting as witnesses at least age 18 who then also sign. Under New York law the Testator doing the Will must also verbally tell witnesses the document is their Will.

LAST WILL AND TESTAMENT

I, _____, of _____, New York do revoke all prior Wills and testamentary documents and do make, publish, and declare this as my Will. I am of sound mind and under no duress or undue influence and acting voluntarily.

1. LIST OF SPOUSE AND CHILDREN. To help show I am mentally competent and have sufficient memory to make a Will I wish to list any living spouse and living children I now have. I currently have the following living spouse and living children:
_____
_____.

2. GIFTS. I give these gifts in this Will, but to get a gift in this section the recipient must survive me except as otherwise stated below.

I give _____ to _____.

I give _____ to _____.

I give _____ to _____.

I give _____ to _____.

I give _____ to _____.

I give _____ to _____.

I give _____ to _____.

I give _____ to _____.

I give _____ to _____.

I give _____ to _____.

3. RESIDUE. I give the rest and residue and remainder of my estate, my money and property of any kind and nature, and anything I have an interest in so long as it was not transferred by other Will provisions, as follows:

   a) to _____ who survive me with persons just named who survive me taking the share of non-survivors, then if anything remains

   b) to _____ and if any of those just named do not survive me their part goes to their lineal descendants per stirpes.

4. ADMINISTRATION. I name, nominate, and appoint _____
as Executor including for me, my Will, and my estate.

5. GUARDIAN. I name, nominate, and appoint _____
to be Guardian of the Person of any minor child of mine and also to have care, authority, custody, and other control of them. I name, nominate, and appoint this same person to be Guardian of Property for any minor child and to have care, control, and power over their property, money, and estate (and if helpful as Conservator and Guardian of the Estate).

6. MISCELLANEOUS. The following applies to this Will and generally.

In this Will no part left unfilled is a mistake including spaces in the residue clause.

The facts support and I want New York state law to apply to this Will and my estate.

If context allows in this Will or other documents the terms Executor and Administrator and Personal Representative are interchangeable. If context allows Conservator and Guardian of Property and Guardian of the Estate and Conservator and Custodian are interchangeable. Any such person has all powers and rights of the others.

I order that my just debts, funeral and related expenses, and taxes be paid as soon after my death as practical but only those items my Executor chooses to pay.

Priority of Will gifts of the same type is based on the order they are written.

The words "give" and "gift" also means a devise, bequest, grant, legacy, or similar.

I am intentionally not providing by Will or other ways for some family, including I am not providing for some children of mine and also children of a deceased child of mine.

If a gift Will reasonably mentions survival then survival is an absolute condition and anti-lapse laws or similar provisions have no effect and without survival the gift lapses. Unless a Will gift specifies otherwise if a Will gift goes to multiple recipients if any do not survive me the part to them lapses and instead goes to other surviving recipients.

No earlier transfer reduces a Will gift unless I usually called it a loan or advancement.

In this Will any gender or gendered word includes all genders, and the singular includes the plural and vice versa, and "they" can mean a single person or many persons.

Unless a Will specifically says otherwise a secured debt including a mortgage or lien shall not be paid off including by an Executor or in probate, and a recipient of a Will gift of property takes it subject to debts. Also, no recipient of property who may lose it or who pays to keep it may have my estate or others pay or do exoneration.

If during my life I disposed of an item in a specific gift then the gift is extinguished (including ademption shall apply and it shall adeem).

I request and authorize any informal, summary, and quick probate or similar action. Any Executor may act independently with no supervision of any court, including independent administration, and with no inventory, appraisal, or other action.

Any Guardian of any type, Conservator, Custodian, or other person managing a minor's property or money may use or invade the principal and sell property without court action.

I give any Executor the a) fullest authority, discretion, and powers allowed by state law, b) power to lease, sell, mortgage, convey, or keep property including real property in a manner and time they deem helpful or proper, and c) authority to settle or pay claims or debts in the time and manner they choose. Any Executor also shall have and possess all powers and authorities conferred by statute or common law in any jurisdiction where Executor may act, including those from the New York Estates Powers & Trusts Law as amended, except for instances which conflict with the express provisions of this Will.

The residue includes lapsed or failed gifts, insurance paid to the estate, digital assets, inheritances owed me, and all I had power of appointment or testamentary disposition over.

Any Executor may access, manage, delete, modify, transfer, and otherwise control any digital accounts and assets I had any interest in or power over.

Any Executor, Personal Representative, Administrator, Guardian of any type like for a person or estate, Conservator, Custodian, and any other fiduciary under this Will or otherwise shall qualify and serve without bond, surety, security, surety bond, or similar.

If evidence does not show it likely a person survived me by 120 hours (5 days) then for this Will and my estate they shall be deemed in all ways as having died before me.

If part of this Will is by law invalid or unenforceable other provisions remain in effect.

Any Executor may at any time transfer money or property of a minor under age 18 to a Custodian to serve under the New York Uniform Transfers to Minors Act or similar law anywhere, and may pick a person to be Custodian including themselves.

TESTATOR

IN WITNESS WHEREOF, I, _____, the Testator, declare I have signed this Will which I do and make voluntarily, on the ____ day of _____, 20____.

_____
Signature of Testator

WITNESSES

The foregoing instrument was signed by the Testator in our presence and declared by the Testator to be the Testator's Will, and we, the Witnesses who sign below, sign our names hereunto to act as witnesses at the request and in the presence of the Testator, and in the presence of each other on the ____ day of _____, 20____.

_____   _____
Signature of Witness #1   Residence Address of Witness #1

_____   _____
Signature of Witness #2   Residence Address of Witness #2

CHAPTER 9
FORM 3: SELF-PROVING AFFIDAVIT

FORM CAN BE DONE TO MAKE USING A WILL LATER EASIER

This form is optional but can be done after a Will is done to help with legal work after a person's death of showing a Will was signed properly so is valid.

FORM SAVES LATER WORK OF SHOWING WILL WAS PROPERLY SIGNED

A Self-Proving Affidavit helps "prove" a Will was signed properly. If this form is not done then after death a little work is need to get evidence from either witnesses to the Will signing, persons familiar with the signatures of people, or a handwriting expert. If this form is not done there is a bit more legal risk a Will isn't followed later. But of people doing Wills about <u>half skip the Self-Proving Affidavit</u> mostly due to hassle of finding a notary on top of 2 witnesses each time a Will is done or re-done, and since it mostly just saves a little later work of people who are happy to do work to get what the Will gives them.

FORM IS DONE BY TESTATOR AND 2 WITNESSES SIGNING BEFORE NOTARY

This form must be signed in front of a person who is a notary (also called a "notary public") by the Testator and 2 witnesses and then the notary notarizes the form. A notary can be found and asked to help at a bank, insurance agent, government office, mail-copying center, and other places. Using a phone book to call a notary and ask if they will help is common. A notary is likelier to help if a person is an existing customer or pays. This form is often done a few minutes after a Will is signed but it can be done much later (even years later) when everyone can meet with a notary. This form can't legally be done before a Will is done. This form when done is often kept paper-clipped to the Will it supports.

SELF-PROVING AFFIDAVIT

STATE OF NEW YORK)
) ss.
COUNTY OF _____)

Each of the undersigned, being duly sworn, deposes and says:

    The foregoing Will was subscribed at the end by _____, the within named Testator in the presence and sight of the undersigned, on the _____ day of _____, 20____, at _____, New York.

    At the time the instrument was subscribed, the Testator declared said instrument to be the Testator's Will.

    The undersigned thereupon signed their names as witnesses at the end of said Will at the request of the Testator, in the presence of the Testator and each other.

    At the time of so executing said Will, the Testator was at least 18 years of age, and in the respective opinions of the undersigned, was of sound mind, memory and understanding, under no constraint, duress, fraud or undue influence, and in no respect incompetent to make a valid Will.

    In the respective opinions of the undersigned, the Testator was able to read, write and converse in the English language, and was not suffering from any defect of sight, hearing or speech, or from any other physical or mental impairment which would affect the Testator's capacity to make a valid Will.

    Each of the undersigned was acquainted with the Testator and makes this affidavit at the Testator's request.

    Said Will was shown to the undersigned at the time this affidavit was made, and was examined by each of them, and such signatures are the signatures affixed by the Testator and by each of the undersigned.

    Said Will was executed as a single, original instrument, and not in counterparts.

_____   _____
Signature of Witness #1   Residence Address of Witness #1

_____   _____
Signature of Witness #2   Residence Address of Witness #2

Severally subscribed and sworn before me on the ____ day of _____, in the year _____.

                                                                  _____
                                                                  Notary Public, State of New York

CHAPTER 10
FORM 4: HEALTH CARE PROXY

FORM CAN NAME HEALTH CARE AGENT AND GIVE INSTRUCTIONS

This form lets a person name someone to make health care decisions if the person is later incapacitated and also write health care instructions. <u>Many people do this 1 popular health care form and skip other forms</u>. But paramedics and others in a hurry usually will <u>not</u> follow this form. This book's form is by the New York Department Of Health, and many websites have a copy of it that can be filled in online and printed. *See https://health.ny.gov/publications/1430.pdf or www.health.ny.gov/professionals/patients/health_care_proxy*. <u>The main part of the form is on the last 2 pages</u> of the 8 page form, and earlier pages are just instructions. This form is often known as a "Health Care Directive".

CAN NAME A PERSON TO BE AGENT TO CONTROL HEALTH CARE IF NEEDED

This form lets a person name someone to be "Health Care Agent" with power to make medical decisions if the person is ever incapacitated. Often named is a spouse, adult child, relative, or friend. Naming a family member can avoid them later having to rush to see a judge to get power to decide things in an emergency. The form has a spot to name a fallback person to act if needed but this is rarely needed so is often skipped.

IN FORM CAN GIVE HEALTH CARE INSTRUCTIONS

In the form people can <u>write health care instructions</u> their Agent, family, and doctors must by law follow. <u>But many people skip written instructions since they are hard to write to cover all situations</u>, these can cause delay or lawsuits if not clear, and people trust the Agent and family to do what is best or what was requested. Family and any Agent should do what person said or wrote was wanted and also use their best judgment. People can name an Agent but skip instructions, or do instructions but not name an Agent. But by law any Agent can only stop artificial fluids or feeding (feeding tube or intravenous IV line) if it is discussed in writing, so a few people write in the form a bit like: "My Agent knows I don't want any artificial nutrition or hydration". Organ Donation can be covered in the form but it is usually best to do this every few years in normal drivers license or state ID forms, and if nothing is said then family can also decide this issue.

PERSON SIGNS FORM WITH 2 WITNESSES

To do the form a person must sign it with 2 persons acting as witnesses who then sign too. The persons who are witnesses must be at least 18 and not a spouse or close family, not be employees of a health care or insurance company involved in care, and not be named Agent in the form. A person can hand the form to their Agent to use when needed or, alternatively, tell people where the form is kept so they can get it later. To cancel the form a person can tell their Agent and maybe also tell places that were shown the form.

Health Care Proxy
Appointing Your Health Care Agent in New York State

The New York Health Care Proxy Law allows you to appoint someone you trust — for example, a family member or close friend – to make health care decisions for you if you lose the ability to make decisions yourself. By appointing a health care agent, you can make sure that health care providers follow your wishes. Your agent can also decide how your wishes apply as your medical condition changes. Hospitals, doctors and other health care providers must follow your agent's decisions as if they were your own. You may give the person you select as your health care agent as little or as much authority as you want. You may allow your agent to make all health care decisions or only certain ones. You may also give your agent instructions that he or she has to follow. This form can also be used to document your wishes or instructions with regard to organ, eye and/or tissue donation.

About the Health Care Proxy Form

This is an important legal document. Before signing, you should understand the following facts:

1. This form gives the person you choose as your agent the authority to make all health care decisions for you, including the decision to remove or provide life-sustaining treatment, unless you say otherwise in this form. "Health care" means any treatment, service or procedure to diagnose or treat your physical or mental condition.

2. Unless your agent reasonably knows your wishes about artificial nutrition and hydration (nourishment and water provided by a feeding tube or intravenous line), he or she will not be allowed to refuse or consent to those measures for you.

3. Your agent will start making decisions for you when your doctor determines that you are not able to make health care decisions for yourself.

4. You may write on this form examples of the types of treatments that you would not desire and/or those treatments that you want to make sure you receive. The instructions may be used to limit the decision-making power of the agent. Your agent must follow your instructions when making decisions for you.

5. You do not need a lawyer to fill out this form.

6. You may choose any adult (18 years of age or older), including a family member or close friend, to be your agent. If you select a doctor as your agent, he or she will have to choose between acting as your agent or as your attending doctor because a doctor cannot do both at the same time. Also, if you are a patient or resident of a hospital, nursing home or mental hygiene facility, there are special restrictions about naming someone who works for that facility as your agent. Ask staff at the facility to explain those restrictions.

7. Before appointing someone as your health care agent, discuss it with him or her to make sure that he or she is willing to act as your agent. Tell the person you choose that he or she will be your health care agent. Discuss your health care wishes and this form with your agent. Be sure to give him or her a signed copy. Your agent cannot be sued for health care decisions made in good faith.

8. If you have named your spouse as your health care agent and you later become divorced or legally separated, your former spouse can no longer be your agent by law, unless you state otherwise. If you would like your former spouse to remain your agent, you may note this on your current form and date it or complete a new form naming your former spouse.

9. Even though you have signed this form, you have the right to make health care decisions for yourself as long as you are able to do so, and treatment cannot be given to you or stopped if you object, nor will your agent have any power to object.

10. You may cancel the authority given to your agent by telling him or her or your health care provider orally or in writing.

11. Appointing a health care agent is voluntary. No one can require you to appoint one.

12. You may express your wishes or instructions regarding organ, eye and/or tissue donation on this form.

Frequently Asked Questions

Why should I choose a health care agent?
If you become unable, even temporarily, to make health care decisions, someone else must decide for you. Health care providers often look to family members for guidance. Family members may express what they think your wishes are related to a particular treatment. Appointing an agent lets you control your medical treatment by:
- allowing your agent to make health care decisions on your behalf as you would want them decided;
- choosing one person to make health care decisions because you think that person would make the best decisions;
- choosing one person to avoid conflict or confusion among family members and/or significant others.

You may also appoint an alternate agent to take over if your first choice cannot make decisions for you.

Who can be a health care agent?
Anyone 18 years of age or older can be a health care agent. The person you are appointing as your agent or your alternate agent cannot sign as a witness on your Health Care Proxy form.

How do I appoint a health care agent?
All competent adults, 18 years of age or older, can appoint a health care agent by signing a form called a Health Care Proxy. You don't need a lawyer or a notary, just two adult witnesses. Your agent cannot sign as a witness. You can use the form printed here, but you don't have to use this form.

When would my health care agent begin to make health care decisions for me?
Your health care agent would begin to make health care decisions after your doctor decides that you are not able to make your own health care decisions. As long as you are able to make health care decisions for yourself, you will have the right to do so.

What decisions can my health care agent make?
Unless you limit your health care agent's authority, your agent will be able to make any health care decision that you could have made if you were able to decide for yourself. Your agent can agree that you should receive treatment, choose among different treatments and decide that treatments should not be provided, in accordance with your wishes and interests. However, your agent can only make decisions about artificial nutrition and hydration (nourishment and water provided by feeding tube or intravenous line) if he or she knows your wishes from what you have said or what you have written. The Health Care Proxy form does not give your agent the power to make non-health care decisions for you, such as financial decisions.

Why do I need to appoint a health care agent if I'm young and healthy?
Appointing a health care agent is a good idea even though you are not elderly or terminally ill. A health care agent can act on your behalf if you become even temporarily unable to make your own health care decisions (such as might occur if you are under general anesthesia or have become comatose because of an accident). When you again become able to make your own health care decisions, your health care agent will no longer be authorized to act.

How will my health care agent make decisions?
Your agent must follow your wishes, as well as your moral and religious beliefs. You may write instructions on your Health Care Proxy form or simply discuss them with your agent.

Frequently Asked Questions, *continued*

How will my health care agent know my wishes?
Having an open and frank discussion about your wishes with your health care agent will put him or her in a better position to serve your interests. If your agent does not know your wishes or beliefs, your agent is legally required to act in your best interest. Because this is a major responsibility for the person you appoint as your health care agent, you should have a discussion with the person about what types of treatments you would or would not want under different types of circumstances, such as:
- whether you would want life support initiated/continued/removed if you are in a permanent coma;
- whether you would want treatments initiated/continued/removed if you have a terminal illness;
- whether you would want artificial nutrition and hydration initiated/withheld or continued or withdrawn and under what types of circumstances.

Can my health care agent overrule my wishes or prior treatment instructions?
No. Your agent is obligated to make decisions based on your wishes. If you clearly expressed particular wishes, or gave particular treatment instructions, your agent has a duty to follow those wishes or instructions unless he or she has a good faith basis for believing that your wishes changed or do not apply to the circumstances.

Who will pay attention to my agent?
All hospitals, nursing homes, doctors and other health care providers are legally required to provide your health care agent with the same information that would be provided to you and to honor the decisions by your agent as if they were made by you. If a hospital or nursing home objects to some treatment options (such as removing certain treatment) they must tell you or your agent BEFORE or upon admission, if reasonably possible.

What if my health care agent is not available when decisions must be made?
You may appoint an alternate agent to decide for you if your health care agent is unavailable, unable or unwilling to act when decisions must be made. Otherwise, health care providers will make health care decisions for you that follow instructions you gave while you were still able to do so. Any instructions that you write on your Health Care Proxy form will guide health care providers under these circumstances.

What if I change my mind?
It is easy to cancel your Health Care Proxy, to change the person you have chosen as your health care agent or to change any instructions or limitations you have included on the form. Simply fill out a new form. In addition, you may indicate that your Health Care Proxy expires on a specified date or if certain events occur. Otherwise, the Health Care Proxy will be valid indefinitely. If you choose your spouse as your health care agent or as your alternate, and you get divorced or legally separated, the appointment is automatically cancelled. However, if you would like your former spouse to remain your agent, you may note this on your current form and date it or complete a new form naming your former spouse.

Can my health care agent be legally liable for decisions made on my behalf?
No. Your health care agent will not be liable for health care decisions made in good faith on your behalf. Also, he or she cannot be held liable for costs of your care, just because he or she is your agent.

Frequently Asked Questions, *continued*

Is a Health Care Proxy the same as a living will?
No. A living will is a document that provides specific instructions about health care decisions. You may put such instructions on your Health Care Proxy form. The Health Care Proxy allows you to choose someone you trust to make health care decisions on your behalf. Unlike a living will, a Health Care Proxy does not require that you decide in advance decisions that may arise. Instead, your health care agent can interpret your wishes as medical circumstances change and can make decisions you could not have known would have to be made.

Where should I keep my Health Care Proxy form after it is signed?
Give a copy to your agent, your doctor, your attorney and any other family members or close friends you want. Keep a copy in your wallet or purse or with other important papers, but not in a location where no one can access it, like a safe deposit box. Bring a copy if you are admitted to the hospital, even for minor surgery, or if you undergo outpatient surgery.

May I use the Health Care Proxy form to express my wishes about organ, eye and/or tissue donation?
Yes. Use the optional organ, eye and/or tissue donation section on the Health Care Proxy form and be sure to have the section witnessed by two people. You may specify that your organs, eyes and/or tissues be used for transplantation, research or educational purposes. Any limitation(s) associated with your wishes should be noted in this section of the proxy. **Failure to include your wishes and instructions on your Health Care Proxy form will not be taken to mean that you do not want to be an organ, eye and/or tissue donor.**

Can my health care agent make decisions for me about organ, eye and/or tissue donation?
Yes. As of August 26, 2009, your health care agent is authorized to make decisions after your death, but only those regarding organ, eye and/or tissue donation. Your health care agent must make such decisions as noted on your Health Care Proxy form.

Who can consent to a donation if I choose not to state my wishes at this time?
It is important to note your wishes about organ, eye and/or tissue donation to your health care agent, or "health care proxy," family members, and the person responsible for disposition of your remains. If you have not already made your wishes to become, or not to become, an organ and/or tissue donor known, New York Law provides a list of individuals who are authorized to consent to organ, eye and/or tissue donation on your behalf. They are listed as follows, in order of priority: your health care agent/proxy; your spouse, if you are not legally separated, or your domestic partner; a son or daughter 18 years of age or older; either of your parents; a brother or sister 18 years of age or older; an adult grandchild; a grandparent; a guardian appointed for you by a court prior to your death; or any other person authorized to dispose of your body.

Health Care Proxy Form Instructions

Item (1)
Write the name, home address and telephone number of the person you are selecting as your agent.

Item (2)
If you want to appoint an alternate agent, write the name, home address and telephone number of the person you are selecting as your alternate agent.

Item (3)
Your Health Care Proxy will remain valid indefinitely unless you set an expiration date or condition for its expiration. This section is optional and should be filled in only if you want your Health Care Proxy to expire.

Item (4)
If you have special instructions for your agent, write them here. Also, if you wish to limit your agent's authority in any way, you may say so here or discuss them with your health care agent. If you do not state any limitations, your agent will be allowed to make all health care decisions that you could have made, including the decision to consent to or refuse life-sustaining treatment.

If you want to give your agent broad authority, you may do so right on the form. Simply write: I have discussed my wishes with my health care agent and alternate and they know my wishes including those about artificial nutrition and hydration.

If you wish to make more specific instructions, you could say:

If I become terminally ill, I do/don't want to receive the following types of treatments....

If I am in a coma or have little conscious understanding, with no hope of recovery, then I do/don't want the following types of treatments:....

If I have brain damage or a brain disease that makes me unable to recognize people or speak and there is no hope that my condition will improve, I do/don't want the following types of treatments:....

I have discussed with my agent my wishes about_____ and I want my agent to make all decisions about these measures.

Examples of medical treatments about which you may wish to give your agent special instructions are listed below. This is not a complete list:
- artificial respiration
- artificial nutrition and hydration (nourishment and water provided by feeding tube)
- cardiopulmonary resuscitation (CPR)
- antipsychotic medication
- electric shock therapy
- antibiotics
- surgical procedures
- dialysis
- transplantation
- blood transfusions
- abortion
- sterilization

Item (5)
You must date and sign this Health Care Proxy form. If you are unable to sign yourself, you may direct someone else to sign in your presence. Be sure to include your address.

Item (6)
You may state wishes or instructions about organ, eye and /or tissue donation on this form. New York law does provide for certain individuals in order of priority to consent to an organ, eye and/or tissue donation on your behalf: your designated health care agent/proxy; your designated agent to control the disposition of your remains; your spouse, if you are not legally separated, or your domestic partner; a son or daughter 18 years of age or older; either of your parents; a brother or sister 18 years of age or older; an adult grandchild; a grandparent; a guardian appointed by a court prior to your death; or any other person authorized to dispose of your body.

Item (7)
Two witnesses 18 years of age or older must sign this Health Care Proxy form. The person who is appointed your agent or alternate agent cannot sign as a witness.

HEALTH CARE PROXY

(1) I, _____

hereby appoint _____
                (name, home address and telephone number)

_____

_____

as my health care agent to make any and all health care decisions for me, except to the extent that I state otherwise. This proxy shall take effect only when and if I become unable to make my own health care decisions.

(2) Optional: Alternate Agent

If the person I appoint is unable, unwilling or unavailable to act as my health care agent, I hereby appoint _____
                (name, home address and telephone number)

_____

_____

as my health care agent to make any and all health care decisions for me, except to the extent that I state otherwise.

(3) Unless I revoke it or state an expiration date or circumstances under which it will expire, this proxy shall remain in effect indefinitely. *(Optional: If you want this proxy to expire, state the date or conditions here.)* This proxy shall expire *(specify date or conditions):*

_____

_____

(4) Optional: I direct my health care agent to make health care decisions according to my wishes and limitations, as he or she knows or as stated below. *(If you want to limit your agent's authority to make health care decisions for you or to give specific instructions, you may state your wishes or limitations here.)* I direct my health care agent to make health care decisions in accordance with the following limitations and/or instructions *(attach additional pages as necessary):*

_____

_____

In order for your agent to make health care decisions for you about artificial nutrition and hydration *(nourishment and water provided by feeding tube and intravenous line)*, your agent must reasonably know your wishes. You can either tell your agent what your wishes are or include them in this section. See instructions for sample language that you could use if you choose to include your wishes on this form, including your wishes about artificial nutrition and hydration.

(5) Your Identification *(please print)*

Your Name _____

Your Signature _____ Date _____

Your Address _____

(6) Optional: Organ, Eye and/or Tissue Donation

I hereby make an anatomical gift, to be effective upon my death, of:
(check any that apply)

☐ Any needed organs, eyes and/or tissues

☐ The following organs, eyes and/or tissues _____
_____

☐ Limitations _____

If you do not state your wishes or instructions about organ, eye and/or tissue donation on this form, it will not be taken to mean that you do not wish to make a donation or prevent a person, who is otherwise authorized by law, to consent to a donation on your behalf.

Your Signature _____ Date _____

(7) Statement by Witnesses *(Witnesses must be 18 years of age or older and cannot be the health care agent or alternate.)*

I declare that the person who signed this document is personally known to me and appears to be of sound mind and acting of his or her own free will. He or she signed (or asked another to sign for him or her) this document in my presence.

Witness 1

Date _____

Name *(print)* _____

Signature _____

Address _____
_____

Witness 2

Date _____

Name *(print)* _____

Signature _____

Address _____
_____

1430   8/22

CHAPTER 11
FORM 5: LIVING WILL

FORM CAN SAY END TREATMENTS IF LATER DOCTORS THINK IT'S USELESS

This form lets a person say to stop certain health care if <u>later</u> doctors think the person is incapacitated and is in bad medical condition and more care likely won't help. <u>Doing this form is serious and usually only the sickest or oldest people do it</u>. But paramedics and others in a hurry usually will <u>not</u> follow a Living Will. There is no 1 standard form for a Living Will, and this book's form is the form by the New York Attorney General found at *https://ag.ny.gov/sites/default/files/livingwill-template-fillin.pdf*. People can type in all their information online or they can complete the form by pen. The New York Senate has a fancier Living Will form at *www.nysenate.gov/sites/default/files/Healthcare%20Proxy%2012.10_0.pdf*.

FORM CAN SAY STOP CARE IF LATER DOCTORS THINK IT WON'T HELP

In the form a person can say to not try most health care if <u>later</u> doctors think an incapacitated person's health is very bad and more care likely won't help. The form has boxes to check to say which care to stop, like whether to not try cardiac resuscitation (pushing on the heart), mechanical resuscitation (pushing air into lungs), artificial nutrition and hydration, and antibiotics. The form has a spot to write instructions but most people skip this. Treatment that may be stopped is often called "life-sustaining" which is different than "comfort care" which is pain medication and pain therapy which usually continues.

PEOPLE SHOULD SIGN FORM WITH TWO WITNESSES

This form is signed by the person doing it in front of 2 persons acting as witnesses who also sign it. A person should use as witnesses some persons at least age 18, who are not named as Agent to control health care for the person, preferably people not involved in a person's healthcare, and preferably not a person who may inherit or financially benefit from a death. Often used as witnesses are family, friends, hospital workers not directly involved in care, or strangers. Once completed the form usually is shown to all places that might give health care so the form is made part of the person's medical file and followed. Many people also keep the form handy so they or their family can show it if needed. To cancel this form a person can clearly say aloud it is canceled and maybe tell places that saw the form that it is canceled.

Instructions for Completing Your New York Living Will

A Living Will **only becomes effective** if you are determined to have a terminal illness or are at the end-of-life and when you are no longer able to communicate your wishes. In New York State, the Living Will was authorized by the courts (not by legislation) so there are no requirements guiding its use. But, a Living Will can serve an important role to provide clear evidence of your wishes.

You can add personal instructions in Item 3 on the form if there are specific treatments that you wish to refuse but are not listed on the document.

You can also add a statement referring to your health care agent such as, "Any questions about how to apply my Living Will are to be decided by my health care agent."

Item 1: Print your name

Item 2: Cross out any of the statements that **do not** reflect your wishes

Item 3: Write in any personal instructions

Item 4: Date and sign the document and include your address

Item 5: Two witnesses must sign the document and print their addresses.

Note: This form does not need to be notarized.

"Completing Your New York Living Will." University of Rochester Medical Center, University of Rochester, 2016, urmc.rochester.edu/MediaLibraries/URMCMedia/jones-memorial/patients-families/documents/living_will_nys.pdf.

New York State Living Will

This Living Will has been prepared to conform to the law in the State of New York, as set forth in the case In re Westchester County Medical Center, 72 N.Y. 2d 517 (1988). In that case the Court established the need for "clear and convincing" evidence of a patient's wishes and stated that the "ideal situation is one in which the patient's wishes were expressed in some form of writing, perhaps a 'Living Will'."

I, [1]_____, being of sound mind, make this statement as a directive to be followed if I become permanently unable to participate in decisions regarding my medical care. These instructions reflect my firm and settled commitment to decline medical treatment under the circumstances indicated below:

I direct my attending physician to withhold or withdraw treatment that merely prolongs my dying, if I should be in an incurable or irreversible mental or physical condition with no reasonable expectation of recovery, including but not limited to: (a) a terminal condition; (b) a permanently unconscious condition; or (c) a minimally conscious condition in which I am permanently unable to make decisions or express my wishes.

I direct that my treatment be limited to measures to keep me comfortable and to relieve pain, including any pain that might occur by withholding or withdrawing treatment. While I understand that I am not legally required to be specific about future treatments **if I am in the condition(s) described above I feel especially strongly about the following forms of treatment**:

[2]
☐ I do not want cardiac resuscitation.

☐ I do not want mechanical respiration.

☐ I do not want artificial nutrition and hydration.

☐ I do not want antibiotics.

However, I **do want** maximum pain relief, even if it may hasten my death.

[3] Other directions:

These directions express my legal right to refuse treatment, under the law of New York. I intend my instructions to be carried out, unless I have rescinded them in a new writing or by clearly indicating that I have changed my mind.

[4]
Signed _____ Date _____

Address _____

I declare that the person who signed this document appeared to execute the Living Will willingly and free from duress. He or she signed (or asked another to sign for him or her) this document in my presence.

[5]
Name of Witness 1 (please print, sign and date)

Signed _____ Date _____

Address _____

Name of Witness 2

Signed _____ Date _____

Address _____

CHAPTER 12
FORM 6: DO NOT RESUSCITATE

IN FORM CAN IMMEDIATELY REFUSE HEALTH CARE

This Chapter actually has 2 forms which are similar and people pick from to do the serious act of saying to immediately no longer try certain health care. Doing this is serious and usually only the sickest or oldest people do it. Both forms are often called the "Do Not Resuscitate" form. These are both official state forms. Both these forms are short and usually will be followed by paramedics and similar personnel.

FIRST FORM SAYS TO IMMEDIATELY NOT TRY MANY KINDS OF CARE

This Chapter's first form, the Medical Orders For Life-Sustaining Treatment form (the "M.O.L.S.T." form), says to immediately not try the many kinds of health care chosen in the form. This form often says to immediately no longer try antibiotics, artificial feeding, and C.P.R. This form is short so it can be read fast and be followed by those in a hurry like paramedics outside a health facility, but this M.O.L.S.T. form is more often used by people who are in a care facility. Pain relief and comfort care is usually still given, so paramedics are still usually called if needed. After doing this form a person is usually free to verbally override it, like by saying a person changed their mind and now do want care to a paramedic or doctor. In recent years the M.O.L.S.T. form has become the main form used to say to immediately no longer try health care, and other forms are less often used including this Chapter's second form.

SECOND FORM SAYS TO IMMEDIATELY NOT TRY RESUSCITATION

This Chapter's second form, the Nonhospital Do Not Resuscitate form says to immediately not attempt resuscitation, which is trying to restart or help breathing or the heart. Resuscitation covers cardio-pulmonary resuscitation (C.P.R.), defibrillation (electric shocks), and machine or tube breathing. This form is short so it can be read fast and followed by those in a hurry like paramedics, and this Nonhospital Do Not Resuscitate form is more often used by people outside a care facility. Pain relief and comfort care is usually still given, so paramedics are still usually called if needed. Note, even after doing form a person is usually free to verbally override it, like by saying to a paramedic or doctor to give all care. Some people also choose to wear a Do Not Resuscitate bracelet made by companies chosen by the state that doctors can help order.

FORM IS SIGNED BY DOCTOR OR SIMILAR AND THEN THE PATIENT

To be valid form these forms must be signed by a person's doctor (physician) or other similar health professional, and by the person doing the form (or their named representative who is authorized to do this). Once the form is done people usually people show it to all places that may give care to add it medical files so it is followed. Usually the person also keeps a copy of the form near their body to show to paramedics or similar personnel who may try to give health care.

NEW YORK STATE DEPARTMENT OF HEALTH

Medical Orders for Life-Sustaining Treatment (MOLST)

THE PATIENT KEEPS THE ORIGINAL MOLST FORM DURING TRAVEL TO DIFFERENT CARE SETTINGS. THE PHYSICIAN/NURSE PRACTITIONER/PHYSICIAN ASSISTANT KEEPS A COPY.

LAST NAME/FIRST NAME/MIDDLE INITIAL OF PATIENT

ADDRESS

CITY/STATE/ZIP

☐ Male ☐ Female

DATE OF BIRTH (MM/DD/YYYY)

eMOLST NUMBER (THIS IS NOT AN eMOLST FORM)

Do-Not-Resuscitate (DNR) and Other Life-Sustaining Treatment (LST)

This is a medical order form that tells others the patient's wishes for life-sustaining treatment. A health care professional must complete or change the MOLST form based on the patient's current medical condition, values, wishes, and MOLST Instructions. If the patient is unable to make medical decisions, the orders should reflect patient wishes, as best understood by the health care agent or surrogate. A physician/nurse practitioner/physician assistant must sign the MOLST form. All health care professionals must follow these medical orders as the patient moves from one location to another, unless a physician/nurse practitioner/physician assistant examines the patient, reviews the orders, and changes them.

MOLST is generally for patients with serious health conditions. The patient or other decision-maker should work with the physician/nurse practitioner/physician assistant and consider asking the physician/nurse practitioner/physician assistant to fill out a MOLST form if the patient:

- Wants to avoid or receive any or all life-sustaining treatment.
- Resides in a long-term care facility or requires long-term care services.
- Might die within the next year.

If the patient has an intellectual or developmental disability (I/DD) and lacks the capacity to decide, the physician (not a nurse practitioner or physician assistant) must follow special procedures and attach the completed Office for People with Developmental Disabilities (OPWDD) legal requirements checklist before signing the MOLST. See page 4.

SECTION A — Resuscitation Instructions When the Patient Has No Pulse and/or Is Not Breathing

Check **one**:

☐ **CPR Order: Attempt Cardio-Pulmonary Resuscitation**
CPR involves artificial breathing and forceful pressure on the chest to try to restart the heart. It usually involves electric shock (defibrillation) and a plastic tube down the throat into the windpipe to assist breathing (intubation). It means that all medical treatments will be done to prolong life when the heart stops or breathing stops, including being placed on a breathing machine and being transferred to the hospital.

☐ **DNR Order: Do Not Attempt Resuscitation (Allow Natural Death)**
This means do not begin CPR, as defined above, to make the heart or breathing start again if either stops.

SECTION B — Consent for Resuscitation Instructions (Section A)

The patient can make a decision about resuscitation if he or she has the ability to decide about resuscitation. If the patient does NOT have the ability to decide about resuscitation and has a health care proxy, the health care agent makes this decision. If there is no health care proxy, another person will decide, chosen from a list based on NYS law. Individuals with I/DD who do not have capacity and do not have a health care proxy must follow SCPA 1750-b.

☐ Check if verbal consent (Leave signature line blank)

SIGNATURE   DATE/TIME

PRINT NAME OF DECISION-MAKER

PRINT FIRST WITNESS NAME   PRINT SECOND WITNESS NAME

Who made the decisions?   ☐ Patient   ☐ Health Care Agent   ☐ Public Health Law Surrogate   ☐ Minor's Parent/Guardian   ☐ §1750-b Surrogate*

SECTION C — Physician/Nurse Practitioner/Physician Assistant Signature for Sections A and B

PHYSICIAN/NURSE PRACTITIONER/PHYSICIAN ASSISTANT SIGNATURE*   PHYSICIAN/NURSE PRACTITIONER/PHYSICIAN ASSISTANT NAME   DATE/TIME

PHYSICIAN/NURSE PRACTITIONER/PHYSICIAN ASSISTANT LICENSE NUMBER   PHYSICIAN/NURSE PRACTITIONER/PHYSICIAN ASSISTANT PHONE/PAGER NUMBER

SECTION D — Advance Directives

Check all advance directives known to have been completed:

☐ Health Care Proxy   ☐ Living Will   ☐ Organ Donation   ☐ Documentation of Oral Advance Directive

*If this decision is being made by a 1750-b surrogate, a physician must sign the MOLST.

DOH-5003 (8/20) p 1 of 4

THE PATIENT KEEPS THE ORIGINAL MOLST FORM DURING TRAVEL TO DIFFERENT CARE SETTINGS. THE PHYSICIAN/NURSE PRACTITIONER/PHYSICIAN ASSISTANT KEEPS A COPY.

LAST NAME/FIRST NAME/MIDDLE INITIAL OF PATIENT DATE OF BIRTH (MM/DD/YYYY)

SECTION E — Orders For Other Life-Sustaining Treatment and Future Hospitalization When the Patient has a Pulse and the Patient is Breathing

Life-sustaining treatment may be ordered for a trial period to determine if there is benefit to the patient. **If a life-sustaining treatment is started, but turns out not to be helpful, the treatment can be stopped. Before stopping treatment, additional procedures may be needed as indicated on page 4.**

Treatment Guidelines No matter what else is chosen, the patient will be treated with dignity and respect, and health care providers will offer comfort measures. *Check one:*
- ☐ **Comfort measures only** Comfort measures are medical care and treatment provided with the primary goal of relieving pain and other symptoms and reducing suffering. Reasonable measures will be made to offer food and fluids by mouth. Medication, turning in bed, wound care and other measures will be used to relieve pain and suffering. Oxygen, suctioning and manual treatment of airway obstruction will be used as needed for comfort.
- ☐ **Limited medical interventions** The patient will receive medication by mouth or through a vein, heart monitoring and all other necessary treatment, based on MOLST orders.
- ☐ **No limitations on medical interventions** The patient will receive all needed treatments.

Instructions for Intubation and Mechanical Ventilation *Check one:*
- ☐ **Do not intubate (DNI)** Do not place a tube down the patient's throat or connect to a breathing machine that pumps air into and out of lungs. Treatments are available for symptoms of shortness of breath, such as oxygen and morphine. (This box should not be checked if full CPR is checked in Section A.)
- ☐ **A trial period** *Check one or both:*
  - ☐ Intubation and mechanical ventilation
  - ☐ Noninvasive ventilation (e.g. BIPAP), if the health care professional agrees that it is appropriate
- ☐ **Intubation and long-term mechanical ventilation, if needed** Place a tube down the patient's throat and connect to a breathing machine as long as it is medically needed.

Future Hospitalization/Transfer *Check one:*
- ☐ Do not send to the hospital unless pain or severe symptoms cannot be otherwise controlled.
- ☐ Send to the hospital, if necessary, based on MOLST orders.

Artificially Administered Fluids and Nutrition When a patient can no longer eat or drink, liquid food or fluids can be given by a tube inserted in the stomach or fluids can be given by a small plastic tube (catheter) inserted directly into the vein. If a patient chooses not to have either a feeding tube or IV fluids, food and fluids are offered as tolerated using careful hand feeding. **Additional procedures may be needed as indicated on page 4.** *Check one each for feeding tube and IV fluids:*
- ☐ No feeding tube
- ☐ A trial period of feeding tube
- ☐ Long-term feeding tube, if needed
- ☐ No IV fluids
- ☐ A trial period of IV fluids

Antibiotics *Check one:*
- ☐ Do not use antibiotics. Use other comfort measures to relieve symptoms.
- ☐ Determine use or limitation of antibiotics when infection occurs.
- ☐ Use antibiotics to treat infections, if medically indicated.

Other Instructions about starting or stopping treatments discussed with the physician/nurse practitioner/physician assistant or about other treatments not listed above (dialysis, transfusions, etc.).

_____

_____

Consent for Life-Sustaining Treatment Orders (Section E) (Same as Section B, which is the consent for Section A)

_____ ☐ Check if verbal consent (Leave signature line blank) _____
SIGNATURE   DATE/TIME

_____
PRINT NAME OF DECISION-MAKER

_____ _____
PRINT FIRST WITNESS NAME   PRINT SECOND WITNESS NAME

Who made the decisions? ☐ Patient ☐ Health Care Agent ☐ Based on clear and convincing evidence of patient's wishes
           ☐ Public Health Law Surrogate ☐ Minor's Parent/Guardian ☐ §1750-b Surrogate*

Physician/Nurse Practitioner/Physician Assistant Signature for Section E

_____ _____ _____
PHYSICIAN/NURSE PRACTITIONER/PHYSICIAN ASSISTANT SIGNATURE* PRINT PHYSICIAN/NURSE PRACTITIONER/PHYSICIAN ASSISTANT NAME DATE/TIME

*If this decision is being made by a 1750-b surrogate, a physician must sign the MOLST.

THE PATIENT KEEPS THE ORIGINAL MOLST FORM DURING TRAVEL TO DIFFERENT CARE SETTINGS. THE PHYSICIAN/NURSE PRACTITIONER/PHYSICIAN ASSISTANT KEEPS A COPY.

LAST NAME/FIRST NAME/MIDDLE INITIAL OF PATIENT DATE OF BIRTH (MM/DD/YYYY)

SECTION F — Review and Renewal of MOLST Orders on this MOLST Form

The physician/nurse practitioner/physician assistant must review the form from time to time as the law requires, and also:
- If the patient moves from one location to another to receive care; or
- If the patient has a major change in health status (for better or worse); or
- If the patient or other decision-maker changes his or her mind about treatment.

Date/Time	Reviewer's Name and Signature	Location of Review (e.g., Hospital, NH, Physician/Nurse Practitioner/Physician Assistant Office)	Outcome of Review
			☐ No change ☐ Form voided, new form completed ☐ Form voided, **no** new form
			☐ No change ☐ Form voided, new form completed ☐ Form voided, **no** new form
			☐ No change ☐ Form voided, new form completed ☐ Form voided, **no** new form
			☐ No change ☐ Form voided, new form completed ☐ Form voided, **no** new form
			☐ No change ☐ Form voided, new form completed ☐ Form voided, **no** new form
			☐ No change ☐ Form voided, new form completed ☐ Form voided, **no** new form
			☐ No change ☐ Form voided, new form completed ☐ Form voided, **no** new form
			☐ No change ☐ Form voided, new form completed ☐ Form voided, **no** new form
			☐ No change ☐ Form voided, new form completed ☐ Form voided, **no** new form
			☐ No change ☐ Form voided, new form completed ☐ Form voided, **no** new form
			☐ No change ☐ Form voided, new form completed ☐ Form voided, **no** new form

THE PATIENT KEEPS THE ORIGINAL MOLST FORM DURING TRAVEL TO DIFFERENT CARE SETTINGS. THE PHYSICIAN/NURSE PRACTITIONER/PHYSICIAN ASSISTANT KEEPS A COPY.

LAST NAME/FIRST NAME/MIDDLE INITIAL OF PATIENT | DATE OF BIRTH (MM/DD/YYYY)

Requirements for Completing the MOLST for Individuals with Intellectual or Developmental Disabilities

Completing the MOLST for individuals with I/DD who lack capacity to make their own health care decisions and do not have a health care proxy:

- The law governing the decision-making process differs for individuals with I/DD. Surrogate's Court Procedure Act (SCPA) Section 1750-b must be followed when making a decision for an individual with I/DD who lacks capacity and does not have a health care proxy.

- MOLST may only be signed by a **physician**, not a nurse practitioner or physician assistant.

- Completion of the **MOLST legal requirements checklist for individuals with I/DD**, including notification of certain parties and resolution of any objections, is **mandatory prior to completion of MOLST**. The checklist is available on the NYS OPWDD website.

- The checklist should be completed when an authorized surrogate makes a decision to **withhold or withdraw life sustaining treatment (LST)** from an individual with I/DD. There are specific medical criteria, included in Step 4 of the checklist. The individual's medical condition must meet the specified medical criteria **at the time the request to withhold or withdraw treatment is made**.

- **Trials** – whether or not a new checklist is required following an unsuccessful trial of LST depends on the parameters of the trial, as specified in Step 2 of the checklist. If Step 2 of the checklist has provided that a trial for LST is to end after a specific period of time or the occurrence of a specific event, it may not be necessary to complete a new checklist following the trial. However, if a trial period is open ended, and the authorized surrogate subsequently decides to request withdrawal of the LST, a new checklist would be required.

- The checklist and 1750-b process apply to individuals with I/DD, regardless of their age or residential setting.

- - THIS PAGE INTENTIONALLY LEFT BLANK - -

NEW YORK STATE DEPARTMENT OF HEALTH

Nonhospital Order Not to Resuscitate (DNR Order)

Person's Name: _____

Date of Birth: _____

Do not resuscitate the person named above.

*Physician/Nurse Practitioner/
Physician Assistant Signature: _____

Print Name: _____

License Number: _____

Date: _____

It is the responsibility of the physician/nurse practitioner/physician assistant to determine, at least every 90 days, whether this order continues to be appropriate, and to indicate this by a note in the person's medical chart. The issuance of a new form is NOT required, and under the law this order should be considered valid unless it is known that it has been revoked. This order remains valid and must be followed, even if it has not been reviewed within the 90-day period.

*For individuals with an Intellectual or Developmental Disability (I/DD), the non-hospital DNR **must** be signed by a physician.

For individuals with an I/DD who do not have capacity and do not have a health care proxy, the physician must ensure compliance with SCPA Section 1750-b.

DOH-3474 (8/20)

CHAPTER 13
FORM 7: STATUTORY SHORT FORM POWER OF ATTORNEY

FORM LETS PERSON SHARE POWER OVER THEIR PROPERTY AND MONEY

This form lets a person during life share power with someone else to let them do things with the person's money, property, debt, and other things. Many people just call this form a "Financial Power of Attorney". The book's form is a statutory form found in law at N.Y. General Obligations Law § 5-1513 and this book's form is copied from the form found at many New York agency websites.

FORM GIVES POWER TO LET SOMEONE CONTROL PROPERTY AND MONEY

This form lets a person (called in the form the "Principal") share power with someone (who is called in the form the "Agent" or "Attorney-in-Fact") to do things to control the person's money, property, and other things. Doing this can let the Agent help and use accounts, pay bills, buy or sell things, sign contracts, hire workers, take out debt, and get information from banks and others. Often named as Agent is a trusted person like a spouse, other relative, or a close friend. The form has room to name a person as "Successor Agent" to act if the first person doesn't, but this is rarely needed and most people skip this. Doing this form might avoid need for more serious options like a guardian, conservator, or nursing home. Note, a person until they are incapacitated can act for themselves or overrule their Agent or fire the Agent. The form is often called "Durable" since power of the form continues even after a person is incapacitated.

IN FORM CAN PICK POWERS AND NAME PERSONS TO MONITOR

Importantly, in the form a person can select which powers are given by initialing certain lines. But usually a person gives all possible powers since they trust the person they named and giving a lot of power may help avoid some legal problems. Also, people can name in the form someone as "Monitor" who an Agent must keep informed about things, but most people skip this since this is extra work and they also trust the Agent.

DUE TO RISKS MANY SKIP THIS FORM OR CONSULT A LAWYER

Many people skip this form or first see a lawyer. Using this form is risky and can lead to harm since the Agent can be wasteful with money, commit fraud or theft, or by carelessness allow some other harms. A person acting as Agent has a duty to be loyal and act reasonably and can be sued for improper actions, but they may later be out of money to pay. Usually banks and others can't be blamed for obeying an Agent. The law is complex and basic acts of an Agent may be fine like paying bills, but some acts may be improper like making gifts, risky investments, or unusual acts. It is best a person not the Agent does anything unusual.

PERSON SIGNS FORM WITH 2 WITNESSES AND A NOTARY

This form is usually signed by a person while they are in front of 2 witnesses who then sign too and in front of a person who is a notary who notarizes and signs as well. This is done on the 4th and 5th page. Sometime later the person getting power in the form should sign the form with a notary, and this is done on the 6th page. The 7th page is usually not used. The form when completed can be kept by a person till needed but often is quickly given to the Agent to hold and use. To cancel the form a person usually tells the Agent it is canceled and takes back copies, and maybe tells all places that saw the form it is canceled.

NEW YORK
STATUTORY SHORT FORM POWER OF ATTORNEY

(a) CAUTION TO THE PRINCIPAL: Your Power of Attorney is an important document. As the "principal," you give the person whom you choose (your "agent") authority to spend your money and sell or dispose of your property during your lifetime without telling you. You do not lose your authority to act even though you have given your agent similar authority.

When your agent exercises this authority, he or she must act according to any instructions you have provided or, where there are no specific instructions, in your best interest. "Important Information for the Agent" at the end of this document describes your agent's responsibilities.

Your agent can act on your behalf only after signing the Power of Attorney before a notary public.

You can request information from your agent at any time. If you are revoking a prior Power of Attorney, you should provide written notice of the revocation to your prior agent(s) and to any third parties who may have acted upon it, including the financial institutions where your accounts are located.

You can revoke or terminate your Power of Attorney at any time for any reason as long as you are of sound mind. If you are no longer of sound mind, a court can remove an agent for acting improperly.

Your agent cannot make health care decisions for you. You may execute a "Health Care Proxy" to do this.

The law governing Powers of Attorney is contained in the New York General Obligations Law, Article 5, Title 15. This law is available at a law library, or online through the New York State Senate or Assembly websites, www.nysenate.gov or www.nyassembly.gov.

If there is anything about this document that you do not understand, you should ask a lawyer of your own choosing to explain it to you.

(b) DESIGNATION OF AGENT(S):

I, _____   _____
       (name of principal)   (address of principal)

hereby appoint:

_____   _____
       (name of agent)   (address of agent)

_____   _____
       (name of second agent)   (address of second agent)

as my agent(s).

If you designate more than one agent above and you do not initial the statement below, they must act together.

(____) My agents may act SEPARATELY.

(c) **DESIGNATION OF SUCCESSOR AGENT(S): (OPTIONAL)**
If any agent designated above is unable or unwilling to serve, I appoint as my successor agent(s):

_____ _____
(name of successor agent) *(address of successor agent)*

_____ _____
(name of second successor agent), *(address of second successor agent)*

If you do not initial the statement below, successor agents designated above must act together.

(____) My successor agents may act SEPARATELY.

You may provide for specific succession rules in this section. Insert specific succession provisions here:

(d) **This POWER OF ATTORNEY shall not be affected by my subsequent incapacity unless I have stated otherwise below, under "Modifications".**

(e) **This POWER OF ATTORNEY DOES NOT REVOKE any Powers of Attorney previously executed by me unless I have stated otherwise below, under "Modifications."**

(f) **GRANT OF AUTHORITY:**
To grant your agent some or all of the authority below, either
    (1)   Initial the bracket at each authority you grant, or
    (2)   Write or type the letters for each authority you grant on the blank line at (P), and initial the bracket at (P). If you initial (P), you do not need to initial the other lines.

I grant authority to my agent(s) with respect to the following subjects as defined in sections 5-1502A through 5-1502N of the New York General Obligations Law:

(____) (A) real estate transactions;

(____) (B) chattel and goods transactions;

(____) (C) bond, share, and commodity transactions;

(____) (D) banking transactions;

(____) (E) business operating transactions;

(____) (F) insurance transactions;

(____) (G) estate transactions;

(____) (H) claims and litigation;

(____) (I) personal and family maintenance: If you grant your agent this authority, it will allow the agent to make gifts that you customarily have made to individuals, including the agent, and charitable organizations. The total amount of all such gifts in any one calendar year cannot exceed five thousand dollars;

(____) (J) benefits from governmental programs or civil or military service;

(____) (K) financial matters related to health care; records, reports, and statements;

(____) (L) retirement benefit transactions;

(____) (M) tax matters;

(____) (N) all other matters;

(____) (O) full and unqualified authority to my agent(s) to delegate any or all of the foregoing powers to any person or persons whom my agent(s) select;

(____) (P) EACH of the matters identified by the following letters _____.

You need not initial the other lines if you initial line (P).

(g) CERTAIN GIFT TRANSACTIONS: (OPTIONAL)

In order to authorize your agent to make gifts in excess of an annual total of $5,000 for all gifts described in (I) of the grant of authority section of this document (under personal and family maintenance), and/or to make changes to interest in your property, you must expressly grant that authorization in the Modifications section below. If you wish to authorize your agent to make gifts to himself or herself, you must expressly grant such authorization in the Modifications section below. Granting such authority to your agent gives your agent the authority to take actions which could significantly reduce your property and/or change how your property is distributed at your death. Your choice to grant such authority should be discussed with a lawyer.

(____) I grant my agent authority to make gifts in accordance with the terms and conditions of the Modifications that supplement this Statutory Power of Attorney.

(h) MODIFICATIONS: (OPTIONAL)

In this section, you may make additional provisions, including, but not limited to, language to limit or supplement authority granted to your agent, language to grant your agent the specific authority to make gifts to himself of herself, and /or language to grant your agent the specific authority to make other gift transactions and/or changes to interests in your property. Your agent is entitled to be reimbursed from your assets for reasonable expenses incurred on your behalf. In this section, you may make additional provisions if you ALSO wish your agent(s) to be compensated from your assets for services rendered on your behalf, and you may define "reasonable compensation."

(i) DESIGNATION OF MONITOR(S): (OPTIONAL)

If you wish to appoint monitor(s), initial and fill in the section below:

(____) I wish to designate _____, whose address(es) is (are) _____, as monitor(s). Upon the request of the monitor(s), my agent(s) must provide the monitor(s) with a copy of the power of attorney and a record of all transactions done or made on my behalf. Third parties holding records of such transactions shall provide the records to the monitor(s) upon request.

(j) COMPENSATION OF AGENT(S):

Your agent is entitled to be reimbursed from your assets for reasonable expenses incurred on your behalf. If you ALSO wish your agent(s) to be compensated from your assets for services rendered on your behalf, and/or you wish to define "reasonable compensation", you may do so above, under "Modifications".

(k) ACCEPTANCE BY THIRD PARTIES:

I agree to indemnify the third party for any claims that may arise against the third party because of reliance on this Power of Attorney. I understand that any termination of this Power of Attorney, whether the result of my revocation of the Power of Attorney or otherwise, is not effective as to a third party until the third party has actual notice or knowledge of the termination.

(l) TERMINATION:

This Power of Attorney continues until I revoke it or it is terminated by my death or other event described in section 5-1511 of the General Obligations Law.

Section 5-1511 of the General Obligations Law describes the manner in which you may revoke your Power of Attorney, and the events which terminate the Power of Attorney.

(m) SIGNATURE AND ACKNOWLEDGMENT:

In Witness Whereof I have hereunto signed my name on _____, 20__

PRINCIPAL signs here: ====> _____

STATE OF NEW YORK)
) ss:
COUNTY OF _____)

On the ____ day of _____, 20__, before me, the undersigned, personally appeared _____, personally known to me or proved to me on the basis of satisfactory evidence to be the individual whose name is subscribed to the within instrument and acknowledged to me that he/she executed the same in his/her capacity, and that by his/her signature on the instrument, the individual, or the person upon behalf of which the individual acted, executed the instrument.

_____
Notary Public

(n) SIGNATURE OF WITNESSES:

By signing as a witness, I acknowledge that the principal signed the Power of Attorney in my presence and in the presence of the other witness, or that the principal acknowledged to me that the principal's signature was affixed by him or her or at his or her direction. I also acknowledge that the principal has stated that this Power of Attorney reflects his or her wishes and that he or she has signed it voluntarily. I am not named herein as an agent or as a permissible recipient of gifts.

_____   _____
Signature of Witness 1   *Signature of Witness 2*

_____ _____
Date   *Date*

_____ _____
Print name   *Print name*

_____ _____
Address   *Address*

_____ _____
City, State, Zip Code   *City, State, Zip Code*

(o) IMPORTANT INFORMATION FOR THE AGENT:

When you accept the authority granted under this Power of Attorney, a special legal relationship is created between you and the principal. This relationship imposes on you legal responsibilities that continue until you resign or the Power of Attorney is terminated or revoked. You must:
   (1) act according to any instructions from the principal, or, where there are no instructions, in the principal's best interest;
   (2) avoid conflicts that would impair your ability to act in the principal's best interest;
   (3) keep the principal's property separate and distinct from any assets you own or control, unless otherwise permitted by law;
   (4) keep a record of all transactions conducted for the principal or keep all receipts of payments and transactions conducted for the principal; and
   (5) disclose your identity as an agent whenever you act for the principal by writing or printing the principal's name and signing your own name as "agent" in either of the following manners: (Principal's Name) by (Your Signature) as Agent, or (your signature) as Agent for (Principal's Name).

You may not use the principal's assets to benefit yourself or anyone else or make gifts to yourself or anyone else unless the principal has specifically granted you that authority in the modifications section of this document or a Non-Statutory Power of Attorney. If you have that authority, you must act according to any instructions of the principal or, where there are no such instructions, in the principal's best interest.

You may resign by giving written notice to the principal and to any co-agent, successor agent, monitor if one has been named in this document, or the principal's guardian if one has been appointed. If there is anything about this document or your responsibilities that you do not understand, you should seek legal advice.

Liability of agent: The meaning of the authority given to you is defined in New York's General Obligations Law, Article 5, Title 15. If it is found that you have violated the law or acted outside the authority granted to you in the Power of Attorney, you may be liable under the law for your violation.

(p)   AGENT'S SIGNATURE AND ACKNOWLEDGMENT OF APPOINTMENT:

It is not required that the principal and the agent(s) sign at the same time, nor that multiple agents sign at the same time.

I/we, _____, have read the foregoing Power of Attorney. I am/we are the person(s) identified therein as agent(s) for the principal named therein.

I/we acknowledge my/our legal responsibilities.

In Witness Whereof I have hereunto signed my name on _____ 20__

Agent(s) sign(s) here: ==>   _____

==>   _____

STATE OF NEW YORK   )
)   ss:
COUNTY OF _____)

On the ____ day of _____, 20__, before me, the undersigned, personally appeared _____, personally known to me or proved to me on the basis of satisfactory evidence to be the individual whose name is subscribed to the within instrument and acknowledged to me that he/she executed the same in his/her capacity, and that by his/her signature on the instrument, the individual, or the person upon behalf of which the individual acted, executed the instrument.

_____
Notary Public

(q) SUCCESSOR AGENT'S SIGNATURE AND ACKNOWLEDGMENT OF APPOINTMENT:

It is not required that the principal and the SUCCESSOR agent(s), if any, sign at the same time, nor that multiple SUCCESSOR agents sign at the same time. Furthermore, successor agents can not use this power of attorney unless the agent(s) designated above is/are unable or unwilling to serve.

I/we, _____, have read the foregoing Power of Attorney. I am/we are the person(s) identified therein as SUCCESSOR agent(s) for the principal named therein.

In Witness Whereof I have hereunto signed my name on _____ 20__

Successor Agent(s) sign(s) here: ==> _____

==> _____

On the _____ day of _____, 20___, before me, the undersigned, personally appeared _____, personally known to me or proved to me on the basis of satisfactory evidence to be the individual whose name is subscribed to the within instrument and acknowledged to me that he/she executed the same in his/her capacity, and that by his/her signature on the instrument, the individual, or the person upon behalf of which the individual acted, executed the instrument.

_____
Notary Public

CHAPTER 14
FORM 8: DESIGNATION OF PERSON IN PARENTAL RELATIONSHIP

FORM LETS PARENT SHARE POWER TO SOMEONE OVER MINOR CHILD

This form lets a parent share power over a minor child under age 18 with someone. This book's form is a copy of a standard form by the Office Of Children And Family Services at the state. At the state webpage is a version of this form that can be filled in online. People can find this form at *https://ocfs.ny.gov*.

FORM CAN DESIGNATE SOMEONE TO HAVE POWER OVER CHILD

A person in a "Parental Relationship" can use this form to "designate" (pick) a person to share power over a minor child under age 18. This can let a friend, relative, teacher, or other person have power to make decisions on a child's health care, school, food, home, or discipline, and this can let them help watch a child. The parent doing the form keeps power and can over-rule any decision and cancel the form. The powers given can be picked, but usually all powers are given to the trusted person to avoid some legal problems. The length of time the form is valid for can be picked, and often 30 days is picked or 12 months is picked. By New York law the form gives no power over adoption, marriage, child's property, and also not over any non-emergency health care (when there is time to communicate with a parent and let them decide). Note, New York also has "standby guardian" form that a person forced to watch child due to parent detention or sickness can themselves sign to get 60 days power.

COMPLETE FORM BY SIGNING OR FOR LONGER POWER USE NOTARY

The form can be completed by 1 parent signing, the 2nd parent signing paragraph 8 if a court order says both parents must agree on health care or school issues (but rarely will a doctor or school check this), and the person given power also must sign. If a person wants the form to be valid for more than 30 days then a notary must also be used for signature. Once the form is completed a parent can keep it till it seems needed, or the form can be quickly given to the person given power to hold and use if ever needed. To cancel the form a person usually tells the person who got power and takes back copies, and maybe tells all places that saw the form.

OCFS-4940 (06/2018)

NEW YORK STATE
OFFICE OF CHILDREN AND FAMILY SERVICES

DESIGNATION OF PERSON IN PARENTAL RELATIONSHIP

Pursuant to section 5-1551 of the New York State General Obligations Law.

1. I, _____, hereby state that I am the parent of the child/children/incapacitated person(s) named below and there are no court orders now in effect in any jurisdiction that would prohibit me from exercising the power that I now seek to authorize.

2. The address and telephone number(s) where I can be reached while this designation is in effect is:

Address:
_____

Telephone: Home ( )   Work ( )
Other ( ) _____

3. I am temporarily entrusting _____, a person over the age of eighteen who resides at _____ New York, _____ telephone number ( ) _____ the care of the following child/children/incapacitated person(s):

NAME:	DATE OF BIRTH:
NAME:	DATE OF BIRTH:
NAME:	DATE OF BIRTH:
NAME:	DATE OF BIRTH:

4. Any authority granted to the person in parental relationship pursuant to this form shall be valid (check appropriate box and initial):

☐ _____ a. for 12 months from the date of signature of this designation, or until the date of revocation, whichever occurs first (must include all parties' addresses and telephone numbers and be signed by all parties in the presence of a notary public); or

☐ _____ b. for 30 days from the date of signature of this designation, or until the date of revocation, whichever occurs first; or

☐ _____ c. from ___/___/___ (date) until and including ___/___/___ (date), or until the date of revocation, whichever occurs first; or

☐ _____ d. commencing upon _____ (state event) and continuing until _____ or until the date of revocation, whichever occurs first.

OCFS-4940 (06/2018)

5. As to the above named child/children/incapacitated person(s), the person in parental relationship named above is authorized to:
(check those that apply)

☐ review school records

☐ enroll in school

☐ excuse absences from school

☐ consent to participation in school program and/or school-sponsored activity

☐ consent to school-related medical care*

☐ enroll in health plans

☐ consent to immunizations*

☐ consent to general health care*

☐ consent to medical procedures*

☐ consent to dental care

☐ consent to developmental screening

☐ consent to mental health examination and/or treatment

* Except as prohibited by Section 2504 of the Public Health Law

Any of the above authorizations may be further limited by conditions defined by the parent, and, if limited, the limitations are written below (e.g., the parent may grant the authority to consent to a mental health examination, subject to the condition that they cannot be reached by telephone or other electronic means).

6. I further authorize the person in parental relationship to request, receive and review, and be granted full and unlimited access to, and obtain complete unredacted copies of any and all of health, medical, financial information and/or any information and/or records as defined in 45 CFR. §164.501 and regulated by the Standards for Privacy of Individually Identifiable Health Information found in 65 Fed. Reg. 82462 as protected private records or otherwise covered under the Health Insurance Portability and Accountability Act of 1996 (HIPAA), Public Law 104-191, for each child/incapacitated person listed in paragraph 3 above. I understand that the information contained in such health and medical records may include information relating to sexually transmitted diseases, acquired immunodeficiency syndrome (AIDS), AIDS-related complex (ARC) and human immunodeficiency virus (HIV), behavioral or mental health services, treatment for alcohol and/or drug abuse and/or addiction. I further understand that I may have access to and/or receive an accounting of the information to be used or disclosed as provided in 45 CFR §164.524, et seq. I further understand that authorizing the disclosure of this health information is voluntary; that I can refuse to sign this authorization. I further understand that any disclosure of this information carries with it the potential for an unauthorized further disclosure of this information by third parties and that such further disclosure may not be protected under HIPAA. In order to induce the disclosing party to disclose the aforesaid private and/or protected confidential information, I forever release and hold harmless said disclosing party who relies upon this instrument from any liability under confidentiality rules arising under HIPAA as a consequence of said disclosure.

7. NOTICE TO PARENTS AND PERSONS IN PARENTAL RELATION: Authorization pursuant to this form is valid until the <u>earlier</u> of revocation by a parent or the date specified in paragraph 4 above. Any parent having signed this designation may revoke such authorization at will, and may notify relevant schools and health care providers of such revocation. A person in parental relationship who receives notification from a parent of such revocation shall forthwith notify any school, health care provider or health plan to which an authorization pursuant to this subdivision has been presented. Failure by the person in parental relation to notify recipients of the authorization or the revocation shall not make notification of revocation by the parent ineffective.

This authorization is temporary, but may be renewed by the parent(s). However, parents and persons in parental relationship involved in a long-term, care-giving arrangement may seek a more permanent legal arrangement by commencing a judicial proceeding to appoint legal guardianship or to determine custody.

OCFS-4940 (06/2018)

(SIGNATURE OF FIRST PARENT)

Note: All signatures below must be notarized if authorization is for a period exceeding 30 days.

Dated: ___/___/_____   (Parent's signature) _____

Sworn to before me this

_____ day of _____ 20 _____

Notary Public _____

(SIGNATURE OF SECOND PARENT – OPTIONAL IN SOME CASES)

8. I, _____, am also the parent of the child/children/incapacitated person(s) named herein, there is a court order directing that both parents must agree on education and/or health decisions concerning such child/children/incapacitated person(s), and I hereby consent to this designation by my signature below.

The address and telephone number(s) where I can be reached while this designation is in effect is:

Address:

Telephone: Home (___) ___-_____   Work: (___) ___-_____
Other: (___) ___-_____

Dated: ___/___/_____   (Parent's signature) _____

Sworn to before me this

_____ day of _____ 20 _____

Notary Public _____

OCFS-4940 (06/2018)

(SIGNATURE OF PERSON GIVEN POWER)

9. I, _____ , the person designated in parental relationship for the child/children/incapacitated person(s) named herein, hereby consent to this designation by my signature below.

Dated: __/__/__   Signature _____

Sworn to before me this

_____ day of _____ 20 _____

Notary Public _____

OCFS-4940 (06/2018)

Instructions for DESIGNATION OF PERSON IN PARENTAL RELATIONSHIP, pursuant to section 5-1551 of the New York State General Obligations Law.

PURPOSE OF THIS FORM:

This form will allow you to designate another person to make medical and educational decisions for your child(ren) or incapacitated person(s) in your care if you can't do so yourself for a specific period of time. This authorization can only be used for a period of up to 12 months. If you will need to have your child(ren)/incapacitated person(s) in the care of someone else for more than 12 months, you may wish to consider other options.

If there is a court order that requires both parents to agree on education and/or health decisions regarding the child(ren), then both parents must sign the form. If not, only one
parent's signature is required.

You keep all of your parental rights with this authorization and can cancel (revoke) this authorization at any time. The person you designate will be able to talk with your child(ren)'s school, teachers and medical providers, and will be able to make routine decisions. The person you designate will not be able to give consent for surgery or other major medical procedures but will be able give consent for routine medical matters. If you do not want the person you designate to be able to make certain decisions, such as decisions concerning immunizations, you can specify that with this form. If the person you designate makes a decision concerning your child(ren)/incapacitated person(s) that you do not agree with, you can override that decision.

The person designated must agree to be "a person in parental authority," and will not be required to assume responsibility for financial support of the child(ren)/incapacitated person(s). Your child(ren) will not have to change their school district if that person resides in another school district. In the event of your death or incapacitation, this designation automatically terminates.

INSTRUCTIONS FOR USING THIS FORM:

Paragraph 1: Fill in your full legal name in the space provided. If there is a court order in effect that requires both parents to sign, the other parent will fill in their name in the space provided in Paragraph 7.

Paragraph 2: Fill in your address and telephone number(s). If this information is not included, the authorization will not be valid for more than 30 days. Use the address where you will be staying during the period this authorization is in effect, even if it is not your legal residence. For example, if this authorization is to be used while you are hospitalized, you would use the hospital's address.

Paragraph 3: Fill in the name, address, and telephone number of the person whom you wish to designate as able to make educational and/or health decisions for your child(ren)/incapacitated person(s). Fill in the name(s) and date(s) of birth for EACH child/incapacitated person.

Paragraph 4: Specify how long you wish this authorization to be in effect by checking the appropriate box and initialing next to it. Remember, you can always revoke (cancel) this designation sooner if you wish. Information about how to do that is included toward the end of these instructions.

- **Use (a)** if you want this designation to be valid for 12 months. If you choose this option, you must provide the address and telephone number for the parent(s) and the other person, and all the signatures must be notarized.

- **Use (b)** if you want this designation to be valid for 30 days. You do not have to include addresses and telephone numbers with this choice, but it is suggested that you do so in the event that medical or educational care providers need to contact you.

- **Use (c)** if you want to use specific dates, for a period of less than or more than 30 days. Remember, this designation cannot be used for more than 12 months, and you must include addresses, telephone numbers, and notarized signatures if you want it to be good for more than 30 days.

- **Use (d)** if you want this designation to begin when something specific, such as in the event you are hospitalized. For this, you write the specific event in the first space provided (example: "When I am admitted to a hospital") and write the date or the event upon which the designation should expire in the second space (example: "30 days later" or "when I am released from the hospital"). Again, you must include addresses, telephone numbers, and notarized signatures if you want it to be good for more than 30 days.

Paragraph 5: List each of the things you wish the person you designate to be able to do. Cross out and initial EACH item that you do NOT wish to allow the person you designate to perform. If there are other things you want to prevent the person from doing, use the blank lines below the list to write those down. For example, if you want to be contacted before any mental health examination is performed, you can write that in the space provided.

Paragraph 6: This paragraph allows the person you designated to have access to your child(ren)'s/incapacitated person(s)' medical records and medical information.

Paragraph 7: This provides some information regarding this form. The parent whose name appears in Paragraph 1 then signs and dates the form. If this authorization is to be in effect for a period of more than 30 days, the signature must be notarized. In this case, you need to take the form to a notary public <u>before</u> you sign it, and sign the form in front of that notary public, who will then also sign the form to indicate that they witnessed your signature. If don't do this, the authorization will automatically expire after 30 days.

Paragraph 8: If there is a court order in effect that requires both parents to agree on education and/or health decisions regarding the child(ren), then the other parent will fill in their full legal name, address, and telephone number in the spaces provided. As with the first parent, they do not have to provide their address and telephone number if the authorization is for a period of 30 days or less, but may wish to. They must provide this information, and sign the form in front of a notary public, if the authorization is to be good for more than 30 days. If there is no court order in effect that requires both parents to agree, you can leave this paragraph blank.

Paragraph 9: Fill in the full legal name of the person to be designated "in parental relationship" to the child(ren)/incapacitated person(s). They then sign and date the form, to show that they agree to be a person in parental relationship. If this authorization is to be good for more than 30 days, they will also need to sign the form in front of a notary public.

OTHER INFORMATION:

- <u>Major medical treatment</u>: The person you designate **CANNOT** give consent for "major medical treatment" which is any medical, surgical, or diagnostic intervention or procedure where a general anesthetic is used or which involves any significant risk or any significant invasion of bodily integrity requiring an incision or producing substantial pain, discomfort, debilitation, or having a significant recovery period. This does not include: any routine diagnosis or treatment such as the administration of medications other than chemotherapy for non-psychiatric conditions or nutrition or the extraction of bodily fluids for analysis; electroconvulsive therapy; dental care performed with a local anesthetic; any procedures which are provided under emergency circumstances, pursuant to section twenty-five hundred four of the public health law; the withdrawal or discontinuance of medical treatment which is sustaining life functions; or sterilization or the termination of a pregnancy.

For example, the person designated can give consent for a child/incapacitated person to have standard dental procedures, such as fillings, but not dental surgery where they would be unconscious during the procedure, such as having their wisdom teeth extracted. A parent's consent will still be required for major medical procedures.

- <u>Revoking this designation</u>: In order to revoke (cancel) the authorization, you simply have to tell the person you designated that you wish to do so, and they are required to notify the appropriate education and medical providers that the authorization has been terminated. While the parent is not required to do this in writing, or to notify the child(ren)/incapacitated person(s) education and medical providers that they have revoked the authorization, they may want to, so that there is no confusion. If two parents signed the form, either parent can cancel the designation by themselves, you do not need both parents.

CHAPTER 15
FORM 9: APPOINTMENT OF AGENT TO CONTROL DISPOSITION OF REMAINS

LETS PERSON BE NAMED TO CONTROL FUNERAL AND ANY CREMATION

This form lets a person name someone to control their funeral, burial, cremation, and all related matters. This book's form is a statutory form found in law at N.Y. Public Health Law § 4201.

IN FORM CAN NAME AGENT TO CONTROL FUNERAL AND RELATED MATTERS

In the form a person can name someone as "Agent" to make decisions about funeral, cremation, burial, and related matters. There is a spot to name fallback persons to act but this is rarely need and often skipped. If this form isn't done closest family control things starting with decedent's spouse, adult children, parents, and then siblings. Most people skip this form and only do it if family will be too upset while mourning, be bad with money, or do unwanted things. The form has a spot to write instructions, but many people skip written instructions and trust their Agent or family to act wisely or follow verbal instructions. People usually should do what the decedent who died wrote or said was wanted so long as the decedent's estate can afford it. The form has areas to fill in to say if pre-purchased funeral services were bought. Payment for things comes from pre-paid funeral accounts, insurance, and the decedent's or estate's money and property, and the Executor and family by law must help arrange payment.

SIGN FORM WITH 2 WITNESSES

The form is signed by a person with 2 persons acting as witnesses who then sign too. A witness can't be someone given power in the form. The completed form should be kept where it can be found very quickly within days of a death, or some people hand it out to someone to hold. The form can be revoked anytime like by throwing it away or clearly telling the Agent it is canceled.

APPOINTMENT OF AGENT TO CONTROL DISPOSITION OF REMAINS
(New York Public Health Law § 4201)

I, _____
(Your name and address)
being of sound mind, willfully and voluntarily make known my desire that, upon my death, the disposition of my remains shall be controlled by
_____.
(name of agent)
With respect to that subject only, I hereby appoint such person as my agent with respect to the disposition of my remains.

SPECIAL DIRECTIONS: Set forth below are any special directions limiting the power granted to my agent as well as any instructions or wishes desired to be followed in the disposition of my remains:
_____
_____
_____
_____

Indicate below if you have entered into a pre-funded pre-need agreement subject to section four hundred fifty-three of the general business law for funeral merchandise or service in advance of need:
[   ] No, I have not entered into a pre-funded pre-need agreement subject to section four hundred fifty-three of the general business law.
[   ] Yes, I have entered into a pre-funded pre-need agreement subject to section four hundred fifty-three of the general business law.
_____
(Name of funeral firm with which you entered into a pre-funded pre-need funeral agreement to provide merchandise and/or services)

AGENT:
Name: _____
Address: _____
Telephone Number: _____

SUCCESSORS: If my agent dies, resigns, or is unable to act, I hereby appoint the following persons (each to act alone and successively, in the order named) to serve as my agent to control the disposition of my remains as authorized by this document:

1. First Successor
Name: _____
Address: _____
Telephone Number: _____

2. Second Successor
Name: _____
Address: _____
Telephone Number: _____

DURATION: This appointment becomes effective upon my death.

PRIOR APPOINTMENT REVOKED: I hereby revoke any prior appointment of any person to control the disposition of my remains.

Signed this ___ day of _____, 20____.

_____
(Signature of person making the appointment)

STATEMENT BY WITNESS (MUST BE 18 OR OLDER) I declare that the person who executed this document is personally know to me and appears to be of sound mind and acting of his or her free will. He or she signed (or asked another to sign for him or her) this document in my presence.

Witness 1: _____
          (signature)
Address: _____

Witness 2: _____
          (signature)
Address: _____

ACCEPTANCE AND ASSUMPTION BY AGENT:
    1. I have no reason to believe there has been a revocation of this appointment to control disposition of remains.
    2. I hereby accept this appointment.

Signed this ___ day of _____, 20____.

_____
(Signature of agent)

APPENDIX:
FILLED OUT SAMPLE LEGAL FORMS

TO GET FORMS TO USE PEOPLE CAN:
   (1) PHOTOCOPY BOOK PAGES,
   (2) TEAR OUT PAGES FROM A BOOK, OR
   (3) DOWNLOAD BOOK WITH FORMS FROM WWW.DAVENPORTPUBLISHING.COM
   AND <u>USUALLY PDF FORM AT IS BEST</u> TO AVOID SPACING/FORMAT CHANGES.

EMAIL ANY COMMENTS TO DAVENPORTPRESS@GMAIL.COM.

On the next pages to show how it can be done are some filled out legal forms which are shown as samples so people can see how it is done.

People can add words to legal forms by computer or typewriter to be neater, but many people just by hand use pen, marker, or pencil to handwrite words into forms.

It is not required but is bit better if signatures are in ink or marker not pencil.

Many parts of the forms especially Will gifts can be left empty and unfilled.

Anyone can fill in words in legal form not just the person doing the form, like a friend who has neat writing can fill in all the words, addresses, and dates that are needed. <u>Only the final signatures must be done by each person who is doing the form.</u>

To add words in form by pen, pencil, typewriter, or computer any of these is fine:
         "I appoint ___*John Doe*___ as Agent",
         "I appoint ___John Doe___ as Agent",
         "I appoint John Doe as Agent".

When doing forms it may help to know "respectively" means "in order just stated".

People need not worry about neatness or small mistakes, and a document is usually fine if those people who knew a decedent in life can tell the likely meaning.

**Sample Filled Out Form: Last Will and Testament (Standard)
with Gifts section skipped to not bother making small gifts**

LAST WILL AND TESTAMENT

I, __Paul Samuel Maxwell__, of __Suffolk County__, New York do revoke all prior Wills and testamentary documents and do make, publish, and declare this as my Will. I am of sound mind and under no duress or undue influence and acting voluntarily.

1. LIST OF SPOUSE AND CHILDREN. To help show I am mentally competent and have sufficient memory to make a Will I wish to list any living spouse and living children I now have. I currently have the following living spouse and living children:

_____ none _____

_____.

2. GIFTS. I give these gifts in this Will, but to get a gift in this section the recipient must survive me except as otherwise stated below.

I give _____ to _____.
I give _____ to _____.
I give _____ to _____.
I give _____ to _____.
I give _____ to _____.
I give _____ to _____.
I give _____ to _____.
I give _____ to _____.

SKIPPED

3. RESIDUE. I give the rest and residue and remainder of my estate, my money and property of any kind and nature, and anything I have an interest in so long as it was not transferred by other Will provisions (all of which is called the "residue"), as follows:

   a) to __Susan Lee Maxwell my sister__ who survive me with persons just named who survive me taking the share of non-survivors, then if anything remains

   b) to __Oscar David Maxwell and Jennifer Judy Tabor__ and if any of those just named do not survive me their part goes to their lineal descendants, per stirpes.

4. ADMINISTRATION. I nominate and appoint __Susan Lee Maxwell__ as Executor including for me, my Will, and my estate.

5. MISCELLANEOUS. The following applies to this Will and generally.

In this Will no part left unfilled is a mistake including spaces in the residue clause.

The facts support and I want New York state law to apply to this Will and my estate.

If context allows in this Will or other documents the terms Executor and Administrator and Personal Representative are interchangeable. If context allows Conservator and Guardian of Property and Guardian of the Estate and Conservator and Custodian are interchangeable. Any such person has all powers and rights of the others.

I order that my just debts, funeral and related expenses, and taxes be paid as soon after my death as practical but only those items my Executor chooses to pay.

Priority of Will gifts of the same type is based on the order they are written.

The words "give" and "gift" also means a devise, bequest, grant, legacy, or similar.

I am intentionally not providing by Will or other ways for some family, including I am not providing for some children of mine and also children of a deceased child of mine.

If a gift Will reasonably mentions survival then survival is an absolute condition and anti-lapse laws or similar provisions have no effect and without survival the gift lapses. Unless a Will gift specifies otherwise if a Will gift goes to multiple recipients if any do not survive me the part to them lapses and instead goes to other surviving recipients.

No earlier transfer reduces a Will gift unless I usually called it a loan or advancement.

In this Will any gender or gendered word includes all genders, and the singular includes the plural and vice versa, and "they" can mean a single person or many persons.

Unless a Will specifically says otherwise a secured debt including a mortgage or lien shall not be paid off including by an Executor or in probate, and a recipient of a Will gift of property takes it subject to debts. Also, no recipient of property who may lose it or who pays to keep it may have my estate or others pay or do exoneration.

If during my life I disposed of an item in a specific gift then the gift is extinguished (including ademption shall apply and it shall adeem).

I request and authorize any informal, summary, and quick probate or similar action. Any Executor may act independently with no supervision of any court, including independent administration, and with no inventory, appraisal, or other action.

Any Guardian of any type, Conservator, Custodian, or other person managing a minor's property or money may use or invade the principal and sell property without court action.

I give any Executor the a) fullest authority, discretion, and powers allowed by state law, b) power to lease, sell, mortgage, convey, or keep property including real property in a manner and time they deem helpful or proper, and c) authority to settle or pay claims or debts in the time and manner they choose. Any Executor also shall have and possess all powers and authorities conferred by statute or common law in any jurisdiction where Executor may act, including those from the New York Estates Powers & Trusts Law as amended, except for instances which conflict with the express provisions of this Will.

The residue includes lapsed or failed gifts, insurance paid to the estate, digital assets, inheritances owed me, and all I had power of appointment or testamentary disposition over.

Any Executor may access, manage, delete, modify, transfer, and otherwise control any

digital accounts and assets I had any interest in or power over.

Any Executor, Personal Representative, Administrator, Guardian of any type like for a person or estate, Conservator, Custodian, and any other fiduciary under this Will or otherwise shall qualify and serve without bond, surety, security, surety bond, or similar.

If evidence does not show it likely a person survived me by 120 hours (5 days) then for this Will and my estate they shall be deemed in all ways as having died before me.

If part of this Will is by law invalid or unenforceable other provisions remain in effect.

Any Executor may at any time transfer money or property of a minor under age 18 to a Custodian to serve under the New York Uniform Transfers to Minors Act or similar law anywhere, and may pick a person to be Custodian including themselves.

TESTATOR

IN WITNESS WHEREOF, I, _Paul Samuel Maxwell_, the Testator, declare I have signed this Will which I do and make voluntarily, on the _8th_ day of _June_, 20_22_.

Paul Samuel Maxwell
Signature of Testator

WITNESSES

The foregoing instrument was signed by the Testator in our presence and declared by the Testator to be the Testator's Will, and we, the Witnesses who sign below, sign our names hereunto to act as witnesses at the request and in the presence of the Testator, and in the presence of each other on the _8th_ day of _June_, 20_22_.

Susan Ann Moon   _14 2nd St., Albany, NY 10022_
Signature of Witness #1   Residence Address of Witness #1

Eve Mable Walker   _35 Buffalo Road, Denver, Colorado 80101_
Signature of Witness #2   Residence Address of Witness #2

**Sample Filled Out Form: Last Will and Testament (Guardian)
with many gifts in Gifts section, Guardian Clause used, and Residue Given By Percentages**

LAST WILL AND TESTAMENT

I, __Paul Brian Baker__, of __Westchester County__, New York, do revoke all prior Wills and testamentary documents and do make, publish, and declare this as my Will. I am of sound mind and under no duress or undue influence and acting voluntarily.

1. LIST OF SPOUSE AND CHILDREN. To help show I am mentally competent and have sufficient memory to make a Will I wish to list any living spouse and living children I now have. I currently have the following living spouse and living children:

_____Ruth May Baker wife_____Oscar Elliot Baker young son_____
_____ Karen Lisa Lundy daughter_____ Derek Rupert Baker son _____.

2. GIFTS. I give these gifts in this Will, but to get a gift in this section the recipient must survive me except as otherwise stated below.

    I give _____big oak table_____ to _____Anne J. Smith_____.
    I give _$5,000_ and _Ford Truck_ to _Loretta Marsha Baxter_.
    I give _buildings, land, and fixtures at 63 Wentworth Road, Rochester, New York,_
        to _Kenneth Alan Ford_.
    I give _all real property and fixtures I own in Nassau County in New York_ to
        Amy Marie Fox and Pamela Sue Fox .
    I give _903 Iceberg Road, Anchorage, Alaska_ to _James Eric Hanson_.
    I give _Irish jewelry and my wedding ring_ to _Mary Natalie Swanson_.
    I give _all jewelry not given above_ to _Kay Baxter and Mary Baxter_.
    I give _$781.35_ to _Mary Natalie Swanson and Kevin Kilby_.
    I give _Wells Fargo acct ending in #8923_ to _Lawrence Deer a hunting buddy_.
    I give _all spare tires and auto parts_ to _Victor Perez my mechanic_.

3. RESIDUE. I give the rest and residue and remainder of my estate, my money and property of any kind and nature, and anything I have an interest in so long as it was not transferred by other Will provisions (all of which is called the "residue"), as follows:

 a) to _____Ruth May Baker_____ who survive me with persons just named who survive me taking the share of non-survivors, then if anything remains

 b) to _45% to Oscar Elliot Baker, and 45% to Karen Lisa Lundy, and 10% to Luis Sanchez my friend_ and if any of those just named do not survive me their part goes to their lineal descendants, per stirpes.

4. ADMINISTRATION. I nominate and appoint ___Ruth May Baker___
as Executor including for me, my Will, and my estate.

5. GUARDIAN. I name, nominate, and appoint ___Amanda Sue Brubaker my sister___
to be Guardian of the Person of any minor child of mine and also to have care, authority, custody, and other control of them. I name, nominate, and appoint this same person to be Guardian of Property for any minor child and to have care, control, and power over their property, money, and estate (and if helpful as Conservator and Guardian of the Estate).

6. MISCELLANEOUS. The following applies to this Will and generally.
   In this Will no part left unfilled is a mistake including spaces in the residue clause.
   The facts support and I want New York state law to apply to this Will and my estate.
   If context allows in this Will or other documents the terms Executor and Administrator and Personal Representative are interchangeable. If context allows Conservator and Guardian of Property and Guardian of the Estate and Conservator and Custodian are interchangeable. Any such person has all powers and rights of the others.
   I order that my just debts, funeral and related expenses, and taxes be paid as soon after my death as practical but only those items my Executor chooses to pay.
   Priority of Will gifts of the same type is based on the order they are written.
   The words "give" and "gift" also means a devise, bequest, grant, legacy, or similar.
   I am intentionally not providing by Will or other ways for some family, including I am not providing for some children of mine and also children of a deceased child of mine.
   If a gift Will reasonably mentions survival then survival is an absolute condition and anti-lapse laws or similar provisions have no effect and without survival the gift lapses. Unless a Will gift specifies otherwise if a Will gift goes to multiple recipients if any do not survive me the part to them lapses and instead goes to other surviving recipients.
   No earlier transfer reduces a Will gift unless I usually called it a loan or advancement.
   In this Will any gender or gendered word includes all genders, and the singular includes the plural and vice versa, and "they" can mean a single person or many persons.
   Unless a Will specifically says otherwise a secured debt including a mortgage or lien shall not be paid off including by Executor or in probate, and a recipient of a Will gift of property takes it subject to debts. Also, no recipient of property who may lose it or who pays to keep it may have my estate or others pay or do exoneration.
   If during my life I disposed of an item in a specific gift then the gift is extinguished (including ademption shall apply and it shall adeem).
   I request and authorize any informal, summary, and quick probate or similar action. Any Executor may act independently with no supervision of any court, including independent administration, and with no inventory, appraisal, or other action.
   Any Guardian of any type, Conservator, Custodian, or other person managing a minor's property or money may use or invade the principal and sell property without court action.
inheritances owed me, and all I had power of appointment or testamentary disposition over.

Any Executor may access, manage, delete, modify, transfer, and otherwise control any digital accounts and assets I had any interest in or power over.

If evidence does not show it likely a person survived me by 120 hours (5 days) then for this Will and my estate they shall be deemed in all ways as having died before me.

If part of this Will is by law invalid or unenforceable other provisions remain in effect.

Any Executor may at any time transfer money or property of a minor under age 18 to a Custodian to serve under the New York Uniform Transfers to Minors Act or similar law anywhere, and may pick a person to be Custodian including themselves.

TESTATOR

IN WITNESS WHEREOF, I, *Paul Brian Baker*, the Testator, declare I have signed this Will which I do and make voluntarily, on the *30th* day of *December*, 20 *21*.

Paul Brian Baker
Signature of Testator

WITNESSES

The foregoing instrument was signed by the Testator in our presence and declared by the Testator to be the Testator's Will, and we, the Witnesses who sign below, sign our names hereunto to act as witnesses at the request and in the presence of the Testator, and in the presence of each other on the on the *30th* day of *December*, 20 *21*.

Olivia Anna Paulson   *82 Forest Road, Lakewood, NY 10188*
Signature of Witness #1   Residence Address of Witness #1

Matthew John Paulson   *82 Forest Road, Lakewood, NY 10188*
Signature of Witness #2   Residence Address of Witness #2

Sample Filled Out Form: Last Will and Testament (Standard) with Will modified to have less gifts and to have a 1 part residue clause

LAST WILL AND TESTAMENT

I, _John David Smith_, of _Westchester County_, New York, do revoke all prior Wills and testamentary documents and do make, publish, and declare this as my Will. I am of sound mind and under no duress or undue influence and acting voluntarily.

1. LIST OF SPOUSE AND CHILDREN. To help show I am mentally competent and have sufficient memory to make a Will I wish to list any living spouse and living children I now have. I currently have the following living spouse and living children:
my adult son Adam Michael Smith.

2. GIFTS. I give these gifts in this Will, but to get a gift in this section the recipient must survive me except as otherwise stated below.

I give _$200_ to _each of my nieces and nephews so about $2,800 in total_.

I give _$400_ to _Garner Food Shelf on Smith Road in the Bronx, New York_.

I give _$340_ to _my old church Sacred Heart in Pueblo, Colorado_.

3. RESIDUE. The rest and residue and remainder of my estate, my property of any kind and nature, and anything I have an interest in, I give to _Adam Michael Smith and Judy Paula Ford_ who survive me and to the lineal descendants per stirpes of a person just named who did not survive me.

4. ADMINISTRATION. I nominate and appoint _Judy Paula Ford my sister_ as Executor including for me, my Will, and my estate.

5. MISCELLANEOUS. The following applies to this Will and generally.
In this Will no part left unfilled is a mistake including spaces in the residue clause.
The facts support and I want New York state law to apply to this Will and my estate.
If context allows in this Will or other documents the terms Executor and Administrator and Personal Representative are interchangeable. If context allows Conservator and Guardian of Property and Guardian of the Estate and Conservator and Custodian are interchangeable. Any such person has all powers and rights of the others.

I order that my just debts, funeral and related expenses, and taxes be paid as soon after my death as practical but only those items my Executor chooses to pay.

Priority of Will gifts of the same type is based on the order they are written.

The words "give" and "gift" also means a devise, bequest, grant, legacy, or similar.

I am intentionally not providing by Will or other ways for some family, including I am not providing for some children of mine and also children of a deceased child of mine.

If a gift Will reasonably mentions survival then survival is an absolute condition and anti-lapse laws or similar provisions have no effect and without survival the gift lapses. Unless a Will gift specifies otherwise if a Will gift goes to multiple recipients if any do not survive me the part to them lapses and instead goes to other surviving recipients.

No earlier transfer reduces a Will gift unless I usually called it a loan or advancement.

In this Will any gender or gendered word includes all genders, and the singular includes the plural and vice versa, and "they" can mean a single person or many persons.

Unless a Will specifically says otherwise a secured debt including a mortgage or lien shall not be paid off including by Executor or in probate, and a recipient of a Will gift of property takes it subject to debts. Also, no recipient of property who may lose it or who pays to keep it may have my estate or others pay or do exoneration.

If during my life I disposed of an item in a specific gift then the gift is extinguished (including ademption shall apply and it shall adeem).

I request and authorize any informal, summary, and quick probate or similar action. Any Executor may act independently with no supervision of any court, including independent administration, and with no inventory, appraisal, or other action.

Any Guardian of any type, Conservator, Custodian, or other person managing a minor's property or money may use or invade the principal and sell property without court action.

I give any Executor the a) fullest authority, discretion, and powers allowed by state law, b) power to lease, sell, mortgage, convey, or keep property including real property in a manner and time they deem helpful or proper, and c) authority to settle or pay claims or debts in the time and manner they choose. Any Executor also shall have and possess all powers and authorities conferred by statute or common law in any jurisdiction where Executor may act, including those from the New York Estates Powers & Trusts Law as amended, except for instances which conflict with the express provisions of this Will.

The residue includes lapsed or failed gifts, insurance paid to the estate, digital assets, inheritances owed me, and all I had power of appointment or testamentary disposition over.

Any Executor may access, manage, delete, modify, transfer, and otherwise control any digital accounts and assets I had any interest in or power over.

Any Executor, Personal Representative, Administrator, Guardian of any type like for a person or estate, Conservator, Custodian, and any other fiduciary under this Will or otherwise shall qualify and serve without bond, surety, security, surety bond, or similar.

If evidence does not show it likely a person survived me by 120 hours (5 days) then for this Will and my estate they shall be deemed in all ways as having died before me.

If part of this Will is by law invalid or unenforceable other provisions remain in effect.

Any Executor may at any time transfer money or property of a minor under age 18 to a Custodian to serve under the New York Uniform Transfers to Minors Act or similar law anywhere, and may pick a person to be Custodian including themselves.

TESTATOR

IN WITNESS WHEREOF, I, __John David Smith__, the Testator, declare I have signed this Will which I do and make voluntarily, on the __21st__ day of __June__, 20__23__.

John David Smith
Signature of Testator

WITNESSES

The foregoing instrument was signed by the Testator in our presence and declared by the Testator to be the Testator's Will, and we, the Witnesses who sign below, sign our names hereunto to act as witnesses at the request and in the presence of the Testator, and in the presence of each other on the __21st__ day of __June__, 20__23__.

__Mark Elliot Potter__   __2 Spruce St, Sherwood, NY 10431__
Signature of Witness #1   Residence Address of Witness #1

__Ann Paula Blom__   __80 Oak Road, Goddard, New York 10872__
Signature of Witness #2   Residence Address of Witness #2

Sample Filled Out Form: Self-Proving Affidavit

SELF-PROVING AFFIDAVIT

STATE OF NEW YORK)
) ss.
COUNTY OF <u>WESTCHESTER</u>)

Each of the undersigned, being duly sworn, deposes and says:

The foregoing Will was subscribed at the end by <u>John David Smith</u>, the within named Testator in the presence and sight of the undersigned, on the <u>21st</u> day of <u>June</u>, 20<u>23</u>, at <u>Yonkers</u>, New York.

At the time the instrument was subscribed, the Testator declared said instrument to be the Testator's Will.

The undersigned thereupon signed their names as witnesses at the end of said Will at the request of the Testator, in the presence of the Testator and each other.

At the time of so executing said Will, the Testator was at least 18 years of age, and in the respective opinions of the undersigned, was of sound mind, memory and understanding, under no constraint, duress, fraud or undue influence, and in no respect incompetent to make a valid Will.

In the respective opinions of the undersigned, the Testator was able to read, write and converse in the English language, and was not suffering from any defect of sight, hearing or speech, or from any other physical or mental impairment which would affect the Testator's capacity to make a valid Will.

Each of the undersigned was acquainted with the Testator and makes this affidavit at the Testator's request.

Said Will was shown to the undersigned at the time this affidavit was made, and was examined by each of them, and such signatures are the signatures affixed by the Testator and by each of the undersigned.

Said Will was executed as a single, original instrument, and not in counterparts.

<u>Mark Elliot Potter</u>   <u>2 Spruce St, Sherwood, NY 10431</u>
Signature of Witness #1   Residence Address of Witness #1

<u>Ann Paula Blom</u>   <u>80 Oak Road, Goddard, New York 10872</u>
Signature of Witness #2   Residence Address of Witness #2

Severally subscribed and sworn before me on the <u>21st</u> day of <u>June</u>, in the year <u>2023</u>.

<u>Nicholas A. Tiffany</u>
Notary

[Notary Seal: NICHOLAS A. TIFFANY, NOTARY PUBLIC, ID Number 02312335668 9623, Comm. Expires Oct 29, 2027, QUALIFIED IN ESSEX COUNTY, STATE OF NEW YORK]

www.ingramcontent.com/pod-product-compliance
Lightning Source LLC
Chambersburg PA
CBHW060414220526
45465CB00008B/2884